Creating with Cattails, Cones and Pods

CREATING WITH CATTAILS, CONES AND PODS

BY DOT ALDRICH

(WITH GEN ALDRICH YOUNG,
WHO ALSO DID THE DRAWINGS)

HEARTHSIDE PRESS INC.
Publishers · Great Neck, New York 11021

Contents

1. MATERIALS, METHODS AND TOOLS

This is a book about the creative and exciting things that you can do using dried plant material. What to gather — where to find it — methods for drying it to preserve its natural beauty — techniques for coloring and shaping the material — all are here. Then easy step-by-step instructions show you how to make animals, dolls, corsages, arrangements, even hats and jewelry, using these same materials.

Find a satisfying hobby in the wonderful world of plants; study the reeds and weeds, the cones, seeds and pods, and as you work with them, be grateful to a bountiful nature for her wonderful gifts.

Most of the materials you will need are yours for the taking — weeds, seeds, pods and cones growing along the country roadsides are a vast creative storehouse hidden from most of the world but easily seen by those with imagination and awareness.

Due to natural variation in size and form, exact measurements cannot be given for plant material. When working out a design, much of the material may be cut lengthwise, crosswise, or trimmed to fit the desired position. At first it might be wise to keep your crafted creatures and flowers realistic; a rose should look like a rose, a lily like a lily, etc. To help achieve a natural look, find pictures or study the actual subject that is being crafted. Children's coloring books are often a good source for pictures. Encyclopedias, bird books, wild or domestic animal books are also helpful. If none is at hand, they may be found in the local library. Later, when you have mastered the technique, you can exaggerate certain features to make some "way-out" creations, if you wish.

It is important to remember that the instructions are not hard and fast rules only suggestions that seemed to the author to be the easiest way to achieve a particular result. Where specific plant materials are mentioned, it is because of certain qualities they possess for that project, such as size, color, form, substance or texture. The plant materials used in these projects are drawn from quite a wide range geographically and you may have difficulty collecting or growing some of them; as, for example, tropical material if you live in the North, and vice versa. When you become familiar with the materials available, it will be easy to make substitutions if you choose the new material with the qualities of the original in mind. If there is an occasional item for which substitutions are difficult, such as luffa sponges for dolls, or raffia, try florist shops, craft and hobby shops or specialty shops handling dried plant materials. Sources of Supply are listed in the back of the book. Your florist shop should be able to supply philodendron leaves or lunaria, and even tape and wire; the hobby shop may supply bunches of raffia (in which, incidentally, there is a tremendous variation in width and length of strands). Once you feel "at home" in your new-found hobby, you will have many happy and sometimes profitable hours working out your own designs.

No one book can hope to list all of the plant material that is suitable for use in arts and crafts. We list only a few of the more common plants to open up a new world of possibilities for you. Once you start seeing what you look at, the habit will grow, and so will your knowledge of this wonderful storehouse of treasures — plant life.

Some of the most beautiful and interesting subjects are very easy to find and are indigenous to most parts of the country. The building up of a collection can be of vital interest to the whole family. Every trip, no matter how short, can be an exciting excursion for new treasures. A list of easily grown annuals and perennials may be helpful in choosing your seeds for next year. Try some of them — they will be delightful additions to your collection of dried material. All on this tiny list are easy to grow.

Annuals: Ambrosia, blue sage, strawberry corn, okra, martynia, radish, onion and garlic, gilia, cuphea and flowering kale.

Perennials: chives, clematis, echinops, yellow centaura, woad (dyer's weed), baptisia, bee balm (monarda) bocconia, physalis, Lenten rose and Christmas rose.

Although some plant materials such as the cattail, thistle, and sycamore have a very wide distribution, not all are readily available in every locality. A good many are worth growing. Brown dock, teasels, Jimson weed, Scotch or bull thistle, ferns, lunaria, poppy pods, hop vine, rudbeckia and martynia would certainly find a place in my garden.

ACORNS: Acorns have two sections, the cap or stem end and the cup, which is actually the seed. There are many varieties of acorns growing all over the country. Some are more than two inches in diameter and some have nearly that length but are much more slender. There are the lovely burr caps that have a fuzzy, ragged appearance and there are smaller caps that have a more or less smooth texture. All acorns are very susceptible to worms and unless they are given an hour or two in a 150° oven as soon as they are gathered, the worms will eat holes through and ruin them.

ALBA POPLAR: Alba poplar is very much improved by using a glycerine solution. The upper side of the leaf is a green so dark that it appears to be black. The underside is white. The leaves should be allowed to stay on the tree until just before a frost. By that time, they will have matured enough so they will not shrivel in drying as the young, immature leaves might do.

BITTERSWEET: Bittersweet, which has many uses (described later), may be gathered along the roadsides in the fall or may be purchased at roadside stands and florists. It is bright orange and very durable.

BROWN DOCK: I know that there are several weeds that I would try to grow if I could not find them elsewhere. The common brown dock is one of them. It is most interesting and useful in its green state, lasting indefinitely in water, and is as decorative in fresh or dried arrangements as a great many of our more exotic garden subjects.

CATTAILS: Everyone is familiar with the cattail. The flower stem should be picked early, i.e., while it is still green, or, at the latest, immediately after it has turned brown. If you wait too long, it starts shedding and disintegrates. There is always a question in my mind whether I should pick it early in the season for my dried arrangements, or leave it until it matures in the fall and then use the stems for all sorts of accessories for the home. (See chapter on Cattails.) Usually I pick a few early. The stems may be trained into graceful curves in the same manner as Scotch broom. These curved cattails will give distinction to any of the arrangements in which they are used.

CORN: A row or two of sweet corn in the vegetable garden will produce dividends far greater than just some mighty good eating. Directions for using corn husks, tassels, etc. appear later in this chapter.

CRABEYE OR ROSARY PEA VINE SEEDS: Crabeyes are a tropic — subtropic subject. They are somewhat egg-shaped and are about a quarter-of-an-inch long and less than that in diameter. Colored a vivid red with one end black (and a small white dot on the black), these are excellent seeds for eyes for dolls or creatures. However, they are in ill repute since they can cause severe illness if crushed and eaten. Crabeye vines grow profusely in the tropics; many items of jewelry, hot-dish mats, and similar objects are made from the seeds by natives of the hot climates. Almost any round or oval seed of the same size could be used as a substitute.

DATE PALM AND COCOS PLUMOSA PALM: Another tropical material is the seed stem of some of the date or cocos plumosa palms. These seed stems can be used in the same manner as Scotch broom. They are a lovely straw color and have a rather interesting texture.

EUCALYPTUS: Australia is the home of several hundred different kinds of eucalyptus, whereas less than fifty varieties grow in the United States (and these are found primarily in the South and in California). Euca pods, as they are commonly called, come in all shapes and sizes, from about four inches in diameter down to a quarter of an inch. Only the smaller ones grow here, but the larger ones may be purchased.

FERNS: In roadside ditches and often found growing in happy juxtaposition with the willows, is the longlasting sensitive fern, which has brown spore cases. Then, nearby, you may find some ostrich ferns. The spore cases of this fern are brown, too, but of a more definite character than the sensitive fern; that is, they are much heavier and have more body. Both of these are gathered in the fall. Cinnamon and royal ferns also yield lovely spore cases. The ones from the cinnamon fern have a particularly appealing rust or cinnamon color and dry in graceful curves. These are ready to pick by mid-June. The sensitive fern and the ostrich fern both have most substantial spore-bearing stems and are easy to grow if they are given a shady place under trees or shrubs or on the north side of a building.

HAZELNUTS AND BEECHNUTS: Hazelnuts before maturity are very

10

useful and interesting if the twig or branch is cut before the nuts have fallen. Beechnuts, on the branch or off, are delightful and different. They can be used in many ways, from corsages to exotic flowers in miniature arrangements.

HOP HORN BEAM, BOX ELDER, SOFT AND HARD MAPLES: All of these produce clusters of winged seed pods that will provide material for a wide range of uses such as dragon flies, to be used on wooden plaques or in mobiles, or multi-petaled flowers to be used on plaques or wired and used in your arrangements of exotic flowers.

HOP VINE: If you have room to grow a vine that will more than repay you in clusters of chartreuse green "flowers", a hop vine is worth the time and trouble it will take to keep it in bounds. It is a rampant climber. The roots are perennial, though the top dies down to the ground every year. Pick the "flowers" early (about August), place the cut stems in a glycerine solution for a few days, and the clusters will dry nicely and be one of the most cherished items in your collection. It is particularly lovely in fresh arrangements.

JIMSON WEED: Jimson weed, while not particularly handsome in the garden, will yield some very interesting and sturdy pods for use in wreaths, plaques, or arrangements.

JUNIPER BERRIES: Juniper berries can also be used as flower centers and have a lovely overall soft blue-grey color.

LUNARIA: Our grandmothers grew and loved the lunaria or money plant. It is an easy-to-grow biennial and usually self-sows to come up year after year. It is also a florists' item. If you buy it, however, you will lose the outer, light-tan scales (since they are peeled off before the florist gets them), so do try to grow some of your own. Cut it while it is still quite green, just as the first pods have a suggestion of tan color rather than green.

MARTYNIA: One of the most interesting and easy-to-grow plants is the martynia or devil's claw, an annual with an extremely rugged pod that will last indefinitely. The flowers are shaped like miniature gloxinias and come in various shades of purple. You will be tempted to use the blooms in arrangements; therefore, grow plenty of them so you can leave some to form pods.

OKRA: This plant may be grown in the flower or vegetable garden. There are several varieties, from a short chubby pod to a long slender one. The pods should be left on the plant until

11

they are quite hard, but haven't split open. If picked too soon, they may shrivel and lose most of their sturdiness.

PEONIES: Single peonies have a very sturdy and unusual seedpod which is dark brown in color. My own peonies have gone to seed for six years or more, and the clumps have grown very rapidly in size. One could not ask for more, or larger, blooms. Evidently, the maturation of the seed does not affect the quality or quantity of the flowers. Most people cut the flower stems off their plants as soon as the blooming season is over — this is a mistake. Some plants, of course, require it, but a great many are not harmed a bit by letting the seedpods mature. It is nature's way of insuring a good crop of plants for next year.

POPPY PODS: Annual poppy seed pods should be picked when they have matured, i.e. just before the pod bursts open and while still green. When dry, the pods will be a variety of greys, some with a greenish cast, some verging onto tan. Perennial poppy pods are also interesting and quite sturdy and are a dark grey-green in color.

ROSE HIPS: Wild or cultivated rose hips, from the smallest to the largest size, will bring a new color to the centers of some of your flowers — or the larger ones may be fashioned into clusters, perhaps to hang over the rim of the container, or for use on a plaque.

RUDBECKIA: Rudbeckia, the purple coneflower, if left till the seeds fall, will be a cone-shaped item with a row of fringe around the stem end of the cone. It is much used for centers of exotic flowers.

RUNNING PINE OR HEMLOCK CANDLES: The candles or pollen-carrying stems of the running pine or hemlock can be carefully clipped from the plant and the cut stems placed in a glycerine solution for several days (see Glycerinizing in Section III). These make wonderful stamens for some crafted flowers. If carefully gathered when the pollen has ripened and blown away, the plant will not be damaged. These may be gathered after the end of August.

SCOTCH OR BULL THISTLE: The bull thistle, in its green state, will delight you with its lavender, sweet-smelling, ball-shaped blossom which is so useful for fresh arrangements. However, it is even more exciting in its dried state: It is best to pick the blossom when it is only half open. Let it lie out of water overnight, then take tweezers and remove the green scales at the base of the flower. Hang the flower to dry. It will fluff out and look like a soft, downy powder puff.

TEASELS: Teasels are another of the handsome roadside plants. When in bloom, they are especially striking with their soft lavender-pink flowers circling the fresh green cone-like seed cases. The teasel's one fault lies in the sharp spines along the entire stem, making handling difficult. Teasels are a biennial which you can grow in the garden but be careful that they do not take over. The plant may grow to six feet tall, and a single plant may have up to two dozen flowers — or later, seed heads. The stems are spiny, so wear gloves when picking them; or carry a piece of sandpaper to rub off the spines before grasping the stem. For most items in this book, the stems are cut short; two inches being more than ample.

WILLOW GALLS: One of the nicest items is the willow gall, which grows on a shrub about the size of a lilac bush and is fairly common in damp ditches along country roads. The gall is about an inch to an inch and a half long and nearly as thick. It is cone-shaped and so near in color to the underside of the leaf that you are very apt to pass it by unless you are familiar with it. It is usually ready to pick after mid-July.

I GATHERING AND STORING PLANTS

All plant material should be picked at the peak of maturity, i. e. before it has weathered. Picking the material at the right time is so important that it may make the difference between successfully drying and preserving it or having it fall apart as you work with it. Also, material that hasn't weathered has a much richer color. One word of caution about picking wildlings — avoid picking those on the conservation list of your state. Conservation lists vary from state to state. As for other materials, when you pick any stem at all, use either shears or a sharp knife to carefully cut the stem. Never *pull* it off or out by the roots. You, or someone else, may wish to pick more from that same spot next year — and leaving the root insures that you can.

You will need space in which to cure and store your collection, and to protect it from excessive dust, mildew, and mice, squirrels and other varments. A corner of the garage or basement, a spare closet or room, or the attic will do. You may even be able to sell your surplus to eager friends or others, or exchange some items with fellow collectors. Your florist will probably be happy to sell or give you one or two large cardboard boxes, of the kind used for shipping flowers. They make excellent storage cases and hold a lot. A handful of mothballs in the boxes will help to protect your collection from hungry varmints. Perhaps a shelf could be put up in the garage to hold the boxes. Be particularly careful of any of the grains such as wheat, barley and oats, for in spite of mothballs, the mice are apt to do a lot of damage to this part of your collection. Peanut butter jars to gallon-size mayonnaise jars will provide good see-through storage for materials such as the cones, seeds and pods. Baby food jars make excellent containers for the smaller items. Be sure everything is dry before putting lids on the jars. A handful of borax in each gallon jar will keep out insects and mold.

II DRYING AND SHAPING

Most plant materials need time to dry and be processed; it may require from one or two days to several months before use. Therefore, you should plan ahead and gather the material when it is in season. For drying purposes, plant materials can be handled as follows: Quite brittle and rather delicate plants can not stand much handling. So, to allow for breakage, more material should be gathered than will be needed. Fairly strong plants can take a reasonable amount of handling. Strong and truly woody plants can stand almost any amount of handling and will last for years. All of these have a place in your work.
Almost all heavy woody things such as cones, acorns, horse chestnuts, etc. will be benefitted by placing them in the oven after you have finished your baking. Lower heat to about 150° (high heat may harm them) and let stand for an hour to thoroughly dry them and rid them of any bugs, worms, insect eggs, or mildew.
For things that require hanging; string up a clothesline of heavy wrapping twine in a convenient place. Wire the stem ends of the material in bunches, leaving extra wire to bend into a hook for hanging. You can use the same clothesline for hanging material that has been lacquered or colored to dry. Remember, all plant material must be thoroughly dry before using; otherwise all the wiring and taping will come loose as the piece shrinks while drying.

14

A great many plants may simply be cut, before they have completely matured; and hung, head down, in a dark, dry place. Cattails and dock are the easiest. They will dry very nicely, keeping a maximum of natural color. Larkspur, zinnia, cockscomb, ambrosia, corn tassels and leaves, goldenrod, tansy and yarrow are a few others that will respond favorably to this treatment.

Pussy willows should be tied in curves before drying by fastening them to coat hanger wire and shaping them to the desired curves or placed in a tall container under a low shelf, so that the tops of the stems bend over. This last way takes less time than tying to a wire, but there will be less variation in curves. Delphinium, blue flax, hydrangeas, liatris, etc., may all be dried this way and, if picked at the proper time, will keep their lovely colors. Delicate grasses, cinnamon fern spore cases, and other weak-stemmed subjects may be laid across the rounded side of a barrel or other similar object. They will droop and acquire a most graceful curve while drying. Oats, barley, wheat and other strong-stemmed material need only be placed upright. Some may be hung head down. All should be allowed to process in a dry, dark place. Never place the subjects in a strong light while drying as the light fades the color.

If you need to shape material that has already dried, soak it in warm water to soften it and then tie it to a heavy wire and shape to your particular needs. Scotch broom has been in use for many years and is one of the easiest materials to shape. Corn tassels and the seed stems of the date or the cocos plumosa palms may also be shaped this way.

DRYING IN BORAX AND CORNMEAL

Use this method to dry and preserve any plant material that loses its color when cut and left to dry naturally. Be sure to cut your flowers while they are at the peak of perfection. They should be free of outside moisture, blemishes and insects. Most autumn leaves will keep their color when this method is used:

Make a mixture of one-third borax and two-thirds cornmeal. Get fairly sturdy, not too deep, corrugated cardboard boxes from your supermarket. Place a few layers of newspaper, paper towels, or an old cotton sheet (folded to fit,) in the bottom of the box. Pour in about an inch of the mixture and lay the flowers or other plant material face up, taking care to keep them from touching each other. The stems should be removed, all but about one-half to one inch. Carefully cover them with the drying medium — no part of the flower should show. Some blossoms such as lily-of-the-valley, lilac, astilbe, etc., cannot, of course, be removed from the stem. Even if you wish to dry the leaves, they should be removed and placed separately in the drying mixture. When completely dry, remove from the mixture and store in a dry place. It is best to keep them either in a covered box or other dark place.

With this particular mixture of borax and cornmeal the subjects can be left untouched for several months and will be in excellent condition when they are finally taken out. There are several other mixtures and materials used by some with a great deal of success: fresh Kitty Litter is one such, and silica gel or Flower-Dri are also used, but are more expensive. Other variations of the cornmeal-borax mixture are (1) sand, borax and cornmeal and (2) one-third salt and two-thirds cornmeal. Salt and sand both have a tendency to cake; therefore they are not as satisfactory as the borax and cornmeal. Too much salt or borax will "burn" some of the color out of the flowers, while too much cornmeal may permit mold to develop. The mixture I use (one-third borax and two-thirds cornmeal) seems to require less checking and gives less trouble than the others.

III GLYCERINIZING

1. *Absorption and Transpiration.* Make a glycerine solution using about one tablespoon glycerine for each scant cup of hot water (120°). Do not use boiling water; about as hot as you can hold your hand in, is sufficient. Varying amounts of glycerine may be used (up to one part glycerine to two parts water), depending on the length of time the material is left in the solution and the nature of the material. Most plant material may be picked and left to dry without further ado. However, a great deal of it will keep better longer and be soft and pliable if the stems are placed in a glycerine solution while they are still green and immature enough to absorb the solution and the leaves are capable of transpiration. In other words, the stem must take up the solution and carry it to the leaves or pods, where the water is then evaporated by the air while the glycerine remains. For this reason it is best to place the container of plant material in the sun or in

a warm, drafty place at first. Plenty of air circulation hastens the absorption process. The container should be kept under cover to avoid getting the material wet by rain or dew. Leave the stems in the solution for several days or longer. Check and add hot solution as the original solution is absorbed. Lunaria, dock, ambrosia and Chinese lanterns, all of which are most successfully preserved by this technique, need a much longer period for absorption than most other items.

Glycerinizing dock needs further details. Be sure to pick dock as soon as it has reached its maximum growth, which in central N. Y. State is in July. Pick some of the type that grows with a very loose head to use for making other flowers. Get it home as soon as you can and make a solution of about one tablespoon of glycerine to one cup of hot water. Cut an inch off the bottom of the stems and place them in glycerine solution. Let it stand for several weeks. Even though the stems are in water, they will dry out. The glycerine makes the dock quite soft and rubbery and much easier to use. Generally dock is quite brittle and tends to shed, unless the glycerine is used.

Some things will change color a great deal when placed in the glycerine solution; some only slightly. You might like to try putting some dye in the solution and allowing the flower stems to absorb it for a day or two before drying. Some materials have a tendency to droop if they absorb too much glycerine. Watchfulness seems to be the only preventative measure, plus a little experience, which is only gained by trial and error. Celosia turns a very soft, lovely brown and becomes very pliable. It may be used to good advantage where you need a drooping effect over the side of the container. Maidenhair fern and lunaria, if placed in this solution and left for a few weeks, will be particularly nice to work with. Both inner and outer scales of lunaria are soft and pliable when treated, and will stand much more handling than if left untreated. They also take on a soft but decided sheen. I much prefer using the treated lunaria.

Stems or branches of leaves such as oak, magnolia, sycamore, jacaranda, silk oak, smoke tree, mahonia and others respond well to this treatment. When placing leafy stems in the glycerine solution, be sure to strip off at least two leaves from the bottom of the stem (more if they are small leaves) and place the stem in the solution deep enough to cover the leaf scars, as this permits greater absorption. Some large leaves will absorb the glycerine better if they are placed singly (not on branches) in the solution. Be sure to cut off the bulge at the end of each leaf stem. This will be less than an inch. The materials should be checked every day. The course of the solution is readily seen and materials should be taken out of the solution as soon as they have processed up to the tips. Then spread them out on newspaper to dry for a few days. They should not be stored in an airtight container nor in a damp place. The hydrangeas, grandiflora and arborescens are good subjects for glycerinizing as is the "smoke" of the smoke tree. Experiment with different subjects.

The "candles" of the running pine or hemlock, when placed in glycerine solution for several days, make wonderful stamens for some flowers. The hop vine responds well to being placed in the glycerine solution for a few days, and the alba poplar is also much improved by it.

Most plant material that has been dried is more or less brittle and difficult to handle without shattering. For those things that need to be more pliable or rubbery, this method is recommended. There will be greater color changes, but the material will be much easier to handle, with considerably less damage to it.

2. *Immersion.* This second glycerine treatment is recommended for foliage where a soft pliable texture is desired, but the stem is too heavy or tough for proper absorption as described in method number one. The texture of lycopodiums and broad-leaved evergreens is much improved with this treatment.

Make a glycerine solution using one-fourth cup glycerine for each cup hot (120°) water. Immerse the entire object in the solution for one to two days. Then hang the soaked object up to dry in an airy place. When storing, do not cover tightly for some time as it may mold if you do.

3. *Brushing* is a third method of applying glycerine. Some materials, such as dried philodendron leaves can be made more pliable by lightly brushing glycerine directly on them. After brushing, stack the leaves one on top of another and wrap them in a plastic bag. Place them in a cool spot for about one week. Check every day for mold. If mold appears, remove the leaves from the plastic bag and spread them out where the air can circulate around them. At the end of the week, remove excess glycerine by wiping each leaf with a soft paper towel. To make sure that they are dry,

18

spread them out on newspaper and let them stand for another two days.

IV PRESSING

The material preserved by this method is usually used to create flower pictures and to decorate stationery, place cards, Christmas cards, etc. All items should be perfect in form and color. No insect or disease spots should be on them, and they should be perfectly clean. A soft paint brush may be used to clean them. For very delicate flowers, I use an infant's hairbrush.

Cut most stems short or completely off. Lay the flowers or leaves flat and face down on a double paper towel. Do not let them overlap. Place a double paper towel on top and weight it down with magazines or other heavy, flat objects. Stack up any number of layers in this manner. They will keep indefinitely. Be sure to keep several thicknesses of paper between each layer. Pansies, violas, primroses, delphinium and daffodils dry beautifully by this method. But that's not true of some of the others like lilies, tulips, and gladioli.

V SKELETONIZING

The process of skeletonizing is used primarily for leaves, which should be perfect and of the desired size. Fully matured leaves are necessary for this process; fresh young leaves will not do. Make a solution of one-half a cake of brown soap and two quarts of water. Boil the leaves in this for thirty minutes. Then remove one leaf and lay it in the sink. Using a stiff vegetable brush, brush the leaf gently. (Running cold water over the work helps.) If the fleshy, green part doesn't brush off easily, boil the leaf for a longer period. A few flecks of solid matter add to the interest of the leaf, so I never brush one entirely free from solids. When all leaves have been brushed, place them in a bleaching solution (Clorox) and allow them to remain until they reach the desired whiteness. They may then be placed in a dye bath of any color, or dried and painted gold or silver, or left white. Be sure that they have dried thoroughly before storing.

VI COLORING AND DYEING

The soft, muted colors of most dried plant material go with a wider range of colors than will the brighter colors of fresh material.

However, if you want bright, vivid colors, fabric dye, food color or water color may be used in several different ways to accomplish the result. The original color of the fresh material may be maintained in the dry state, or it may be changed to a different color.

To maintain original color place the stems of the freshly cut material in a dye solution that exactly matches its natural color. The dye will be absorbed and when dried, the flower will maintain this color.

Dye added to warm water will also be absorbed into the flower through the stem. Tansy, yarrow and goldenrod are excellent for this process.

To change color of dried material, the quickest and easiest way is simply to apply florist's spray or dye without regard to the original color of the material used. Gold or other metallic finishes that are in use during the holidays and for other special occasions can also be easily applied. For leaves or other items where a definite color is needed, various shades of liquid shoe polish are the answer. Brush it on sparingly as it may be too heavy a color otherwise. Always have the material clean and thoroughly dry before using the shoe polish. Flax fibers may be dyed by following the directions on a package of fabric dye.

To restore color to plant material that has lost its color in drying, or faded more than is desirable, place it in a dye solution of the original color. It can also be sprayed with florists' spray.

FOR CLEAR LACQUER FINISHES

Do any trimming or shaping first, then clean the material carefully. Spray it thoroughly with a clear plastic, acrylic or lacquer spray. This does not change color or texture; it simply removes the lifeless look and points up hidden color. It does not produce a high gloss, and it makes the object less apt to shed dust and particles on the area where it stands. Cones and other woody items are made stronger by dipping them in white shellac, slightly thinned varnish or lacquer. If dipped after they have been wired, they may be hung to dry by bending the end of the wire stem over to make a hook. Any of these transparent coatings may be applied by spraying, brushing, or dipping, as a means of preserving, strengthening, or finishing most items.

VII PREPARING CORN

Virtually every part of the corn plant has some craft value, even the stalk itself. Cut it to suitable length, peel the leaves back to the joint, and use the stalk as the highest placement in a fresh arrangement.

Dry the leaves and use them as is or cut down into smaller leaves, or use them to make bows for corsages.

Corn tassels may be used somewhat like Scotch broom. Cut the tassel off the stalk as soon as the silk on the ear shows signs of drying. Lay the tassel in a glycerine solution for a day or two (see section III, this chapter) and then, using soft string or old cotton strips, tie it in curves over a coat hanger bent to the desired shape. Hang it to dry in a sheltered place. Save plenty of tassels and spray some with gold, silver or other color for your Christmas decorations.

The corncob, too, after the kernels have been eaten, may be used in several ways. After they are dry, they may be broken down into smaller sections and used in arrangements or in wreaths. (Red cobs are particularly nice.) You may cut off half-inch slices and make flowers and corsages out of them.

Cornhusks may also be used to make flowers, and of course, cornhusk dolls. Save all the husks you can get from the ears of corn. Remove them from the ear and spread them out to dry. Depending on the climate, it may take several weeks (more or less) for them to dry completely.

After the cornhusks have been dried and you are ready to use them for a project, they will be easier to handle if they are dampened again. Lay the husks in a pan of hot water (add glycerine if more flexibility is desired) for fifteen minutes or less. Remove and wrap in a towel. Keep them in a towel until they are needed.

The reason for not using *fresh* husks is that there is considerable shrinkage in drying and also there is the danger of mildew in the finished item. Once dried, husks take less time to dry again.

VIII PREPARING WHOLE FRUIT

When drying fruit such as apples, lemons, oranges, osage oranges, etc., push a florist's pick into the fruit at the stem end while it is still fresh. Leave about one inch sticking out, then when it has dried you will have a very sturdy stem to attach to wire in case it is needed. After the fruit has dried, it is almost impossible to add such a stem without an electric drill. Try sticking an apple, lemon or orange full of whole cloves, add a florist's pick for a stem, and let it dry. Then use the "pomander" as a focal point in an arrangement. It will give off a nice spicy fragrance for a long time.

IX   PREPARING FERNS AND LUNARIA

Ferns and brakes of all kinds, while more fragile than most of the material, can be made a little less brittle by placing the crushed stems in a glycerine solution (See section III in this chapter.) This should be done immediately after picking them. Allow them to stay in the solution for a few days, then remove and press them flat between newspapers or other absorbent materials. Place a weight on top and leave it there about a week so the ferns won't curl out of shape. Some ferns will keep their green color and some will turn brown; be sure to pick enough so that you will have plenty of each color.

If lunaria is picked when green, it may be glycerinized to make it less fragile in its dry state. Once lunaria has dried, however, it is not possible to use glycerine to condition it since it will no longer draw moisture up into its stem. In this event, shellac will make the scales a little less fragile. Spread them out on a newspaper and shellac one side. Let dry, perhaps overnight. Turn them over, shellac the other side and let dry.

X   TREATING DRIFTWOOD

Remove any branchlets or twigs that interfere with good design and check to see if the item can be secured in the desired position before processing it. All branches, driftwood, fungi, and other woody plant materials should be brushed thoroughly with a stiff brush to remove any dust, dirt, or loose particles. Absolute cleanliness of any material used is a must. If sanding is needed, use one of the finer sandpapers unless there is a great amount of deposit to be removed, in which case, use the coarse paper first and finish with the fine.

1. *Shoe Polish or Dye*: when applied with a light hand, can give a branch or piece of driftwood a glow and vibrancy lacking in

the grey-looking material that has weathered too long, or not long enough.

2. *Paste Floor Wax*: Often a coat or two of paste floor wax with a brisk brushing between coats can make the wood much more alive looking and also make it partly waterproof and less of a dust catcher.

3. *Clear Plastic Spray*: A quicker and easier way is to clean the object thoroughly and then give it one or two coats of clear plastic or acrylic spray. This is called grooming.

4. *Bleach*: Driftwood or any of the woody plant materials may be bleached by immersing in a strong bleach solution after they have been carefully cleaned. Some of the plastic baby or pet bathtubs make fine vessels to hold the bleach solution. If a deep vessel is needed, there are plastic pails, wastebaskets, or garbage containers that will take care of every need. When the object is removed from the bleach, rinse it with clear water, and if possible, hang it to dry. Be sure that it is absolutely dry before you use it. Plastic spray is not necessary and usually is not desirable on bleached items.

XI HOLDING DRIFTWOOD IN POSITION

There are several methods of holding heavy branches firmly.

1. *Wooden Base*: One way is to use a wooden base at least one inch in thickness and of adequate size to look well with the branch or driftwood. Place it on the base where it is to be staged and mark the points where it rests on the base. It may need more than one anchor to hold it firmly. Drill holes a quarter of an inch in diameter at as many marked points as is necessary. Then drill holes up into the corresponding position of the branch or driftwood. Glue quarter-inch dowels into the base and set the branch on top, with holes and dowels matching. It may be glued in place if desired.

2. *Needlepoint Holders*: Another method is to purchase screw-on needlepoint holders of the right size for the wood being used. These holders have a hole and a screw in the middle which fastens the needlepoint holder to the bottom of the wood. It is an excellent way to hold even large branches firmly in place.

3. *Styrofoam Base:* A two-inch thick piece of styrofoam may be used as a base for dried arrangements or driftwood. One need only push ends or other supports down into the styrofoam and

it will be secure for quite a while if the arrangement is not handled roughly. Of course, the base should be painted to harmonize with the other materials. Paint will quite often cause styrofoam to disintegrate; to avoid this, cover the styrofoam with a coat of shellac, brushing it on carefully to give good coverage. Then paint or spray over the shellac after it is dry.

XII   MATERIALS TO BE BOUGHT

Materials to buy, other than those from the plant world, are relatively few and inexpensive: florist's wire and picture-cord wire, pipe cleaners, florist's tape, ribbon, nylon net, shellac, clear plastic spray, cement or glue, thread, some medium fine and medium coarse grit sandpaper, some tufts of cotton, and perhaps some glitter for Christmas decorations. Materials will be repeated in future chapters, for specific projects.

WIRE: It is sold by the pound or bunch at five-and-dime stores and at hobby and craft shops. The best size wire for the widest range of materials is #28. A half-pound each of #18, #22, #28 and #30 wire will handle most of your needs.

The higher the number of the wire, the finer it will be. Perhaps the finest in florist's wire is #32, but it is not easily found. An excellent substitute is a roll of picture-cord wire, which may be purchased in either silver or copper color. This wire is composed of several very fine strands braided together to form a thick strong cord, so that a small roll will last a long time. To use, cut it in six-inch lengths or longer (twelve inches will probaby be the maximum) and separate by pulling out the strands one by one. Do not attempt to unravel it; it will pull out quite readily after the first strand has been removed. These strands will take care of any of the fine wiring for delicate stemmed items you will make. The #18 wire will be strong enough for most projects, and where one wire does not have sufficient rigidity, two or more wires can be used. Never use too heavy a wire as it will not hug the stem tightly and may break it. Remember, two lightweight wires will hold tighter than one heavy wire when wound around the stem of your plant material. Use *one* wire at a time. Add the second only if it is needed. When using more than one wire in a place, it is good to tape each wire for an inch or two, or for its full length if greater bulk is needed. This taping holds the wires together so they will not slip out of place. The tape acts as a bond since it will stick to itself.

Thin, wire coat hangers will provide heavier wire if it is needed, but this wire is not as flexible as florist's wire. Another substitute for a heavy gauge florist's wire (if you live on a farm) is baling wire, which is used for baling hay and straw. For instructions for wiring and taping plant material, see chapter V *Strange Flowers*.

PIPE CLEANERS: A package of pipe cleaners may be purchased at cigar stores, stationers, or five-and-dime stores. Due to their texture, pipe cleaners or chenille stems have greater holding power than the bare or covered wire when inserted and glued into drilled holes.

FLORIST'S TAPE: "Floratape" is a good brand of florist's tape, and may be purchased in five-and-dime stores or craft and hobby shops. It would be wise to have one of each of the basic colors of tape — green, brown and white — then, when making corsages especially, you will have a selection. This is one of the materials that will be needed in almost every project, so it is not itemized in the list of materials at the beginning of each project.

Be sure your plant material is completely dry, since Floratape will not stick to wet materials.

Half-inch strips of crepe paper may be substituted for the tape, if necessary, but it is more difficult to use and is much less satisfactory. If you should use crepe paper, be sure to fasten the ends securely with cement.

RIBBON AND NYLON NET: Various ribbons and nylon netting are used in some projects, but it would probably be wise to check through the projects you will be working on before buying ribbon.

SHELLAC, LACQUER, CLEAR PLASTIC SPRAY, VARNISH: All of these are possible finishes to enhance and protect the dried materials.

CEMENT OR GLUE: A tube of hobby cement or a bottle of glue is also available almost anywhere. Either one is okay, but the hobby cement usually dries faster. In places where cement might not hold on a smooth surface, a wisp of cotton placed between both surfaces and saturated with the cement will help to hold both together. Another bond stronger than cement alone is made by mixing a bit of talcum powder with the cement.

When holes are drilled for cemented-in wires, make the hole a little larger than the diameter of the wire. The cement is placed over the hole, then the wire is used to work it down into the hole and left to dry in place. Sometimes a wisp of cotton placed over the cement and worked into the hole with the wire will help to catch and hold the wire firmly.

THREAD: A spool of cotton thread, size 40-50, is useful for binding or temporarily holding material where tape would be too bulky.

XIII   TOOLS AND WORK AREA

All the tools required to start you off on these projects can be acquired for an initial investment of five dollars or less, and the children or relatives could be encouraged to give any of them as a Mother's Day, birthday or Christmas gift.

Sharp shears, razor blades, a linoleum knife — all are invaluable as cutting tools for your work. In addition to the cutting tools, you will need a pair of long-nosed pliers, a pair of tweezers, some clip clothespins, pin-curl clips, a ruler, a dressmaker's awl or an ice pick for punching holes, a pencil with a soft lead, and a paint brush with bristles about an inch-and-a-half long (for grooming and cleaning material). A bead needle, which is useful for stringing soft seeds, may be purchased in hobby shops. Almost any fine-toothed saw may be used, but a small key-hole saw will cut most things and should cost less than a dollar.

It is necessary to have a means of drilling holes in hard material such as nuts, driftwood, and some seedpods. A hobby drill makes all your drilling problems very simple, but it may be expensive. If it is out of the question, perhaps you have access to a regular wood-working electric hand-drill which can be held in a drill stand. This would be a good second choice. If you're not so lucky, then you'll just have to work a little harder; an ice pick or a darning needle may be used for piercing holes in most items. For heavy or woody material, it may be necessary to heat the pick to burn the hole through.

If all of your tools, wire and other necessary items are in one place, it will be more of an incentive to start and finish a project than if you have to locate everything before getting to work. A basket, roughly the size of a large shoe box, with a lid, will serve nicely as a workbox. If no basket is available, a large shoe box, reinforced with a covering of contact paper, will do the trick. Put all your tools and materials in the workbox, and when you start to work, spread an old sheet over the working area or work on newspapers as an aid to cleaning up later. It is well worth the initial effort to have all of the working units together in one convenient place.

2. CATTAIL MAGIC

Have you ever noticed the many cattails growing along the road-sides and on low, marshy ground? They cover miles of swamp and marshland and are one of the few plants that have worldwide distribution.

Have you wondered if they had any practical or ornamental value? They have both. The roots are rich in starch, may be eaten like a potato, and also produce fiber. The fluff, or down, has been used in life jackets, baseballs, and mattresses. The pollen is highly inflammable and in many places in India and Europe it is used for tinder. The leaves are used to make baskets and rush seats for chairs. These are only a very few of the practical uses for the cattail, none of which are of much immediate use to the average housewife.

However, the decorative uses are just as numerous and will appeal to anyone interested in handicraft — and what woman isn't interested in making something new, intriguing, and beautiful with little expenditure of money, effort, and time?

Experiments with cattail stems have resulted in a collection of accessories for the home which are both useful and decorative, cost little or nothing to make, and are a pleasure to create and use.

Maybe I should say that it was love at first sight between me and the cattail; actually, the chance remark of a friend started the whole thing. We were in her barn where she stored her collection of unusual branches, fungi, seedpods, and other things that are any veteran flower-arranger's stock-in-trade. I noticed a bunch of tall, straight stalks completely unfamiliar to me in one corner. "What in the world are those?", I asked. With a laugh she answered, "Oh, that's my cattail timber." That's when it happened. It was as if I were looking at cattails for the first time. I had never seen them without their thick, brown tops, but now I marveled at their slender, sturdy stems, which were from four to six feet long.

All the way home I looked at the cattails growing near the road. I was astonished to realize how many there were, and the phrase "cattail timber" kept running through my mind. Later that evening my eyes wandered to a bamboo mat I was using under a flower arrangement. I had often thought I could make a better one. Suddenly I knew what "cattail timber" was; it was the material that would enable me to make a better mat and an unlimited variety of other items. I excitedly began making the mat. The stems were easy to work with because I could run a darning needle through them when I wanted to bind them, and I found I had all the tools I needed: shears, razor blade, ruler and a darning needle. The work went fast and I was pleased with the results.

The next time I was demonstrating flower arrangement, I used my new mat and mentioned that it was made from cattail stems. After the talk I was amazed at the interest it had aroused. "Where did you get it?" someone asked. "You made it! Oh, I wish I were talented so I could make one too." I knew that no special talent was needed and offered to show her how to do it. Soon, with very little instruction, this woman and many others were working with cattail timber.

I devised a number of projects that anyone could build with cattail timber. Then one day someone said to me, "After you leave, I forget some of the instructions you gave us. If only I had a book to follow, I could work alone".

So here is the book, your cattail timber is waiting to be picked, and the few tools you'll need are probably already in your house. Now your fun with the cattail is about to begin.

Materials Used in Cattail Projects

CATTAIL STEMS. Pick them in the fall, preferably after the first heavy frosts, when they are fully mature and have reached their maximum size and strength. You can find them in marshy land just about everywhere. Cut the stems as close to the ground as possible. Do not pull out by the roots or you will destroy the plant, and when you go back to look for cattails next year, they won't be there.

Break off the top just below the brown flower head. If you do not remove it, the fuzz will be all over everything when it dries. Store in your garage or cellar, or any place where they will not be exposed to the weather or moisture. If they get wet, they will weaken and rot. Store until they are completely dry; it will take as little as two weeks to as long as all winter, depending on how warm and dry the storage place is. It is necessary to go through this curing process so that the piece you make will not shrink and loosen after you have finished it.

After curing, remove leaves from stems. If leaves are removed when green, they will rip down the full length of the stem, leaving a mark. If they are dry, they will break off neatly. Start with the bottom leaf, pull it down to where it joins the stem and pull off. Take the next leaf, and do likewise, etc. It goes rather quickly once you have learned how to do it.

Before using stems, sand them lightly with a fine-grain sandpaper (#0) to remove the slight rough spots where the leaves were.

The easiest way to cut the stems is with a sharp razor blade, Fig. 1 (A). Put the stem on a table and press the razor blade through the stem. (Remember, you may cut into the table top too so work on a surface you don't care about.) Some pieces look better with stems that are cut straight, others with ends cut at a slant. Throughout this book reference is made to the large- and small-diameter end of the stem, (B). As the cattail grows, the part of the stem nearest the ground is thicker than the top.

In building with stems, take care not to group all the large ends together, except in cases where you might require one side of the object to be longer than the other. Occasionally you will want to add variety and interest to a piece by using split stems, (C); that is, a large-diameter stem which has been split lengthwise. To do this, stand the stem on end and press razor blade slowly down through it. However, this procedure requires a great deal of patience and a firm hand, so it is used infrequently.

RAFFIA. This soft, pliable plant fiber is used as string; it matches color of cattail stem. You can find it in hobby-craft shops, florists, seed and garden supply houses. Moisten raffia before using; this makes it much easier to handle. If you need longer lengths of raffia, tie shorter strands together as you work. The joinings can be concealed between two cattail stems.

COTTON RUG YARN, STRING, STRONG EMBROIDERY COTTON, CARPET WARP. All are possible substitutes for raffia, and may be used to introduce a note of color. Sewing supply or yarn shops have all of these.

WIRE (#12 THROUGH #26), PICTURE CORD WIRE. Fine soft wire used by florists for delicate or temporary binding in corsages, 12″ or 18″ lengths. You can buy it in florist and some hobby shops. Whenever you use wire to hold cattail stems together, first pierce a hole in the stem with a darning needle where you want the wire to go through.

SHELLAC, VARNISH OR PAINT. Use shellac to waterproof stems; varnish may be substituted. Or, if you prefer, you may paint the pieces made from cattail stems instead of using shellac or varnish, though most people prefer the natural finish.

Every piece must be shellacked, varnished or painted. Give each piece two coats of either. For the first coat, dilute shellac with alcohol or varnish with turpentine—two parts varnish or shellac and one part turpentine or alcohol. Apply generously. This first coat will soak deeply into the stems and make them strong and waterproof. Let piece stand for about two days or until thoroughly dry. For the second coat, use shellac undiluted. This gives the surface a hard, resistant, protective coating. You can buy any or all of them at paint or hardware stores.

Fig. 1. Working with cattail stems

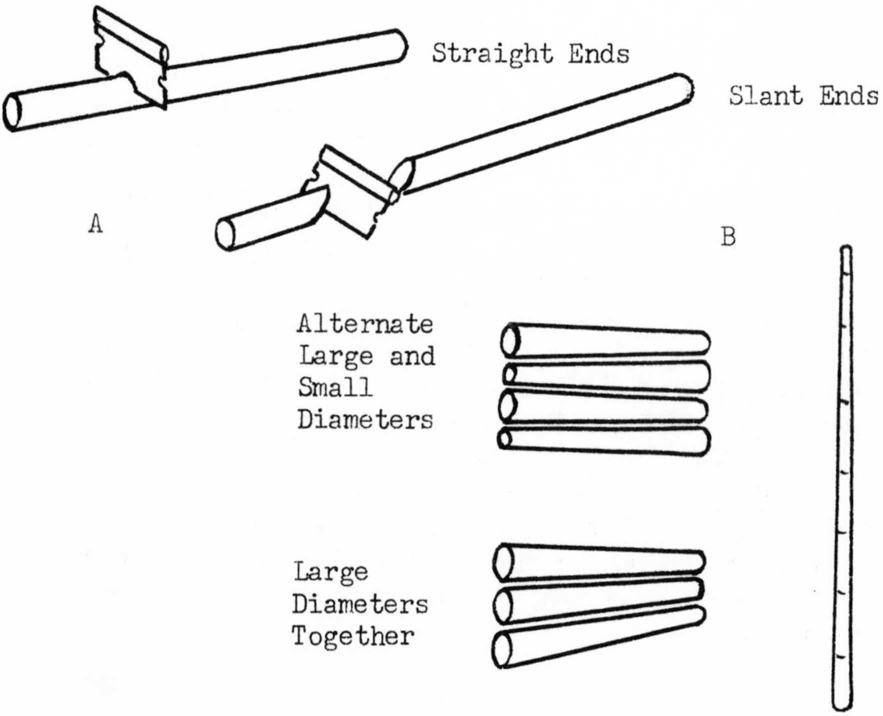

Straight Ends

Slant Ends

A

B

Alternate
Large and
Small
Diameters

Large
Diameters
Together

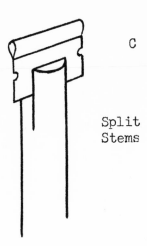

C

Split
Stems

SMALL CONES for ornamental use in some projects. From florist shop or the nearest evergreen tree, hemlock, larch, etc.

SPLINT. A tough, fibrous, flexible ½″ strip used for baskets and chair seats. From hobby shops, seed and garden supply houses.

WIRE CIRCLES. Used by florists in making wreaths. From florist shop.

SCREENING. Copper is preferable; it doesn't rust and color is good with cattails. From hardware store.

STYROFOAM. White plastic material, usually sold in blocks, in five-and-dime stores.

BALSA WOOD. Very soft, fine-grained wood, easily cut with sharp knife. From hobby shops.

Tools Required

Tools used in most projects: Sharp knife, razor blade (single edge), scissors, pencil, tweezers, ruler or yardstick, tape measure, 1″ flat paint brush, 2 large darning needles (must have eyes big enough to thread raffia), clip clothespins, and pin-curl clips, the latter two being used as clamps.

Tools used in only one or two projects: Thumbtacks; paper clips; small, round (#4) watercolor brush; needle-nosed pliers with wire cutter; brace and bit, or small electric drill; ice pick; small fine-toothed saw.

CATTAIL SERVING TRAY

The sturdy 12″ x 18″ tray with matching jackets for glasses will provide a unique decorative note at your next patio picnic, (See Plate 1; Figs. 2 and 3.)

31

Materials Needed

> 30 cattail stems (approximately)
> Raffia, heavy (or double strands), moistened
> Acorns or small cones, for decoration

STEP 1. From large ends of cattail stems cut 4 pieces 12" long, for handles, and 8 pieces 18" long, for braces; from small or middle sections cut 65 pieces 12" long.

STEP 2. The 18" stems are the braces. Temporarily wire two of them together in the middle. Tie a long piece of raffia near one end of these braces so that both ends of the raffia are of equal length, (B).

STEP 3. Set one of the small diameter 12" stems across the braces so that it extends ½" beyond one edge. Cross the raffia over it and under the braces as shown, (C).

STEP 4. Set another stem beside the first one. Pull the raffia up between the two stems, and again cross it over the 12" stems and under the braces. Push these two stems close together and tighten the raffia — you will have two stems bound in position. (D). Bind in 12" stems until the entire length of the braces is covered. Tie the raffia underneath at the end, and cut it off. (Make sure you don't put all the large diameter ends along one edge of the tray.)

STEP 5. Now do the other edge of the tray. Take two more 18" braces, put them in position under the stems (½" in from edge) and bind each 12" stem to them in the same way as you did the first edge.

STEP 6. The remaining four braces must be fastened on top of the tray, (E). in this manner: Thread a darning needle on each end of a long piece of raffia. Start at a point 5" in from the end of the brace and push both darning needles up between the cattail stems, (F). Using the same cross-stitch as before, bind this brace in place out to the end. Do not cut the raffia. Secure all four corners in this way.

STEP 7. To add the handles and ornaments take two of the 12" large-diameter stems. Set them across the two braces on top of the tray and bind them in place with the raffia that is still hanging from each corner, (G). Put the handle on the other end in the same way. For ornaments, wire small cones or acorns at each corner. Varnish (see directions at beginning of chapter).

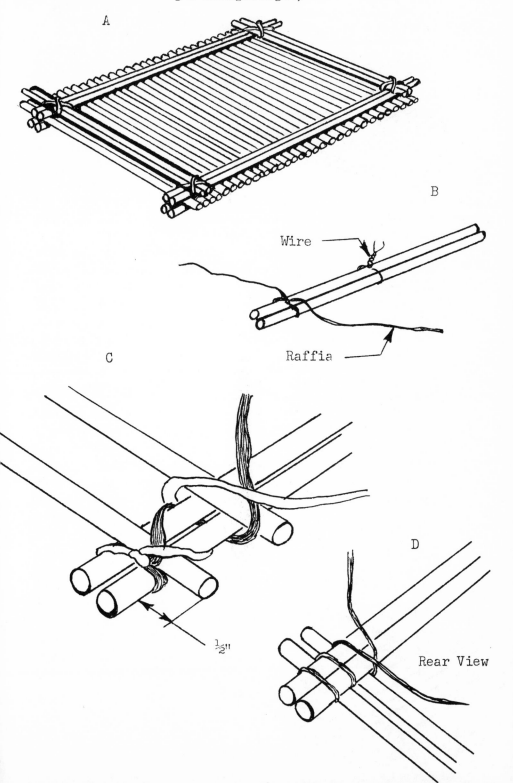

Fig. 2. Starting serving tray

A

B

Wire

Raffia

C

D

Rear View

$\frac{1}{2}''$

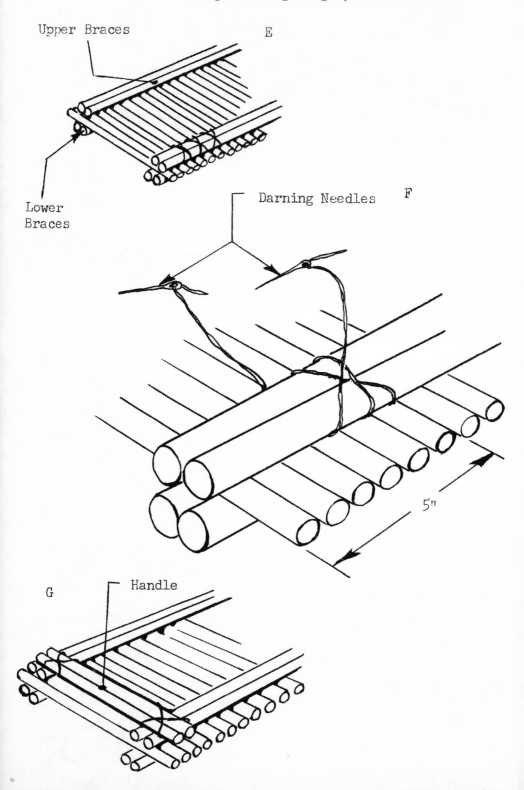

Fig. 3. Finishing serving tray

Upper Braces

E

Lower
Braces

Darning Needles

F

5"

Handle

G

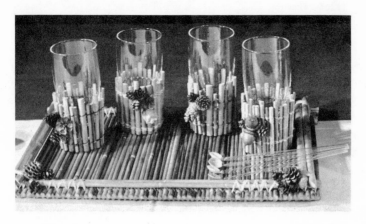

Plate 1.

JACKET FOR GLASS

The following makes a jacket approximately 3″ in diameter and 3½″ high. (See Plate 1, Figs. 4 and 5.)

Materials Needed

> 4 to 6 cattail stems
> #18 florists' wire
> Picture cord wire
> Raffia, moistened
> Floratape

STEP 1. MAKE WIRE FRAME. Using #18 wire, make a circle around a glass, (B). Slide the circle off the glass, allow it to loosen slightly, and wire it closed with a piece of picture cord wire. Make another wire circle for the top of the glass (slightly larger for a tapered glass). Then tape both circles with Floratape.

STEP 2. CUT CATTAIL STEMS: Using small or tip ends, no more than ¼″ in diameter, cut approximately 20 pieces 3″ long. From stems no larger than ⅜″ in diameter, cut five pieces 3½″ long. Split these five larger stems in half lengthwise with a razor blade to make ten pieces. Arrange all the stems flat on a table as shown in (C). Mark each stem with a pencil ½″ from the end. Be sure to keep the spaces between the split stems equal by proper arrangement of the small stems, as in (D).

STEP 3. To make jacket, take the smaller wire circle and tie a length of raffia tightly to it near the end of the wire joining, (E). This circle will be near the bottom of the jacket. In (C)

35

the first stem is marked #1. Place this stem on the wire circle so that the ½" mark is on the wire. Tie it into position with the raffia. Take the #2 stem and bind it into position with the raffia, making sure the ½" mark is on the wire, (F). Bind all stems to the wire circle in the same way, except that on the last stem tie the two raffia ends together. Do not cut them off. Stand the jacket on the table and make whatever adjustments are necessary to make it stand evenly.

STEP 4. Tie a piece of raffia to the larger wire circle as you did to the first circle. Set the wire circle inside the ring of cattail stems, ½" down from top of short stems. The joined part of this circle will be on the opposite side from the joining of the other circle, (G). Tie raffia around the cattail stem it is nearest to. On the opposite side of the jacket, temporarily secure one stem to the wire circle by twisting a piece of wire around it. Thread a large darning needle with long end of the raffia that is already tied to one cattail stem (H). Bind all the stems to the top wire circle, using the same binding stitch as before, (F). The darning needle is used so that you can keep the stems close together while you are binding them to the wire circle. Keep checking and adjusting as you bind this circle into position as stems sometimes have a tendency to slant and slide out of position. When all the stems are bound to the circle, tie the raffia ends together as you did on the bottom circle, and cut the raffia off close to the stem.

STEP 5. MAKE BOTTOM AND ORAMENTS. Thread a large darning needle with the raffia end extending from the lower wire circle. Before using the raffia to weave with, twist it so that it is cord-like, rather than a flat strip. Weave the raffia back and forth between the cattail stems making sure to go both above and below the wire circle, (I). In weaving, when you come to the end of the raffia, tie another length to the one you are working with, twist it, and continue weaving. On completion of weaving, tie raffia to one of the cattail stems and snip it off short. If you wish to ornament the jacket, a cluster of small cones (blue spruce or hemlock), acorns, or any other dry material may be wired to the front. Each jacket may have a slightly different ornament to give it individuality; ornaments can be changed for the occasion or season. Varnish.

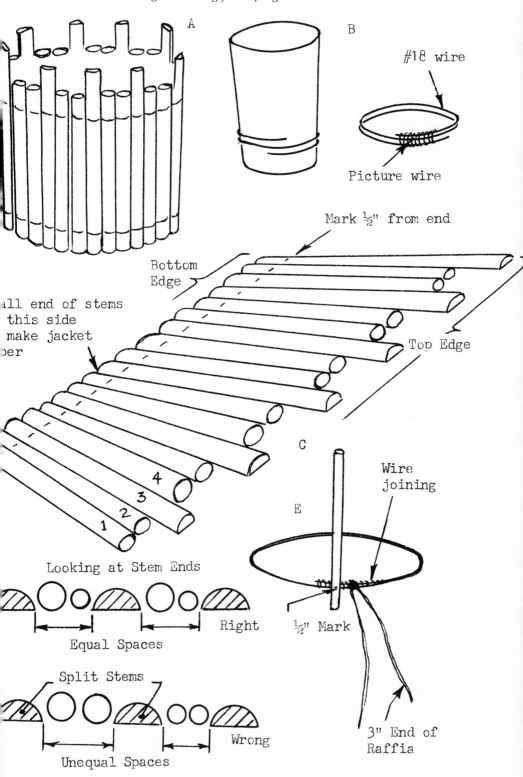

Fig. 4. Starting jacket for glass

A

B

#18 wire

Picture wire

Mark ½" from end

Bottom Edge

Top Edge

all end of stems
this side
make jacket
er

4
3
2
1

Looking at Stem Ends

Equal Spaces

Right

Split Stems

Unequal Spaces

Wrong

C

E

Wire joining

½" Mark

3" End of Raffia

Fig. 5. Finishing jacket for glass

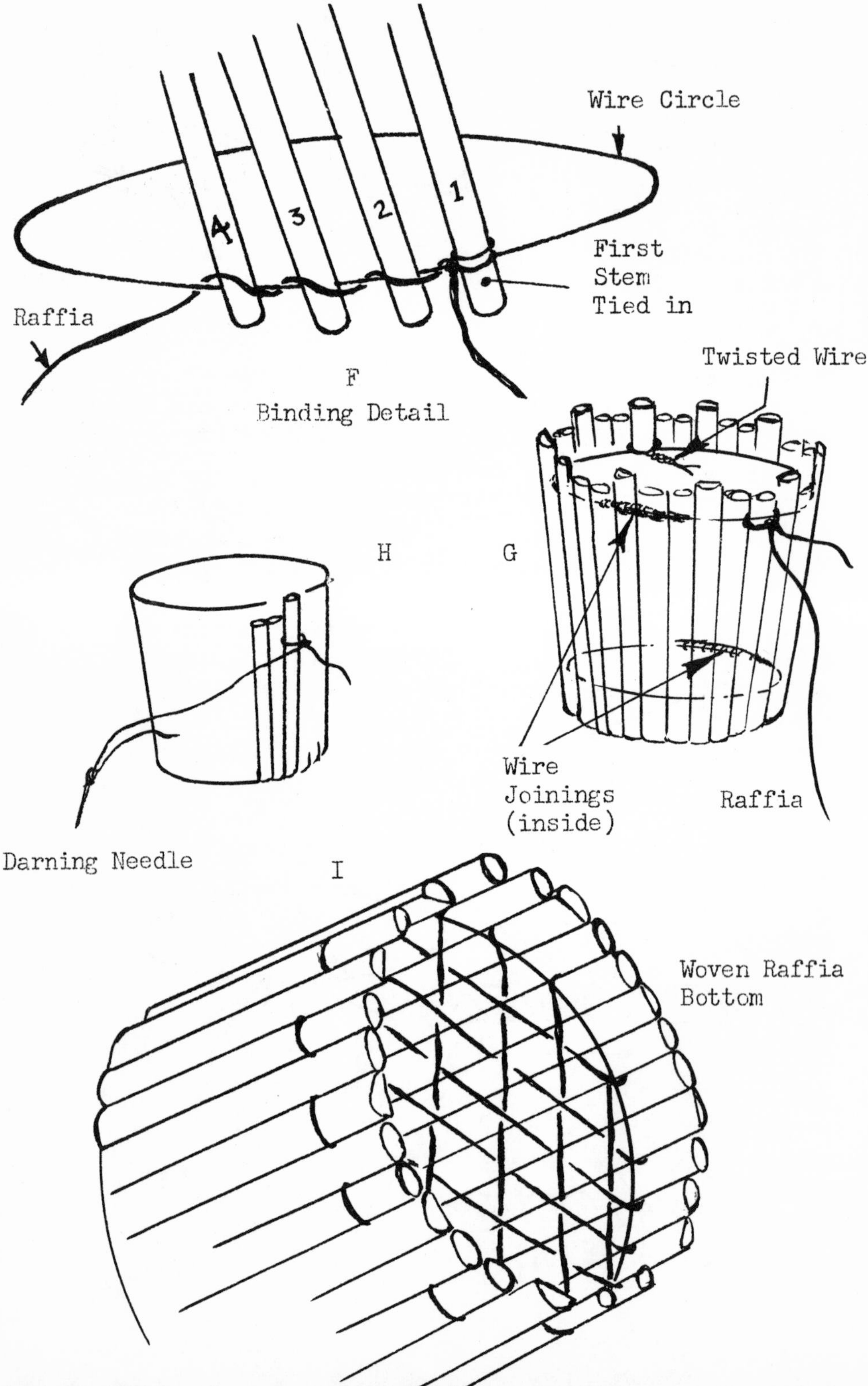
Wire Circle
4
3
2
1
First Stem Tied in
Raffia
F
Binding Detail
Twisted Wire
H
G
Wire Joinings (inside)
Raffia
Darning Needle
I
Woven Raffia Bottom

BUN BASKET

Perfect for serving hot rolls or bread, this basket stands 6″ high with a top diameter of 10″, tapering down to 5″ at the bottom. (See Figs. 6 and 7).

Materials Needed

    6 to 8 cattail stems
    Raffia, heavy (or double strands), moistened
    2 heavy wire circles, 5″ and 8″ in diameter (from an old or inexpensive
      lampshade)
    Picture cord wire
    Cones or acorns, for decoration
    Shellac or varnish

STEP 1. PREPARE CATTAIL STEMS: Cut approximately 45 pieces 6″ long. Use the entire cattail stem in this project, both the largest and smallest diameter parts. For handles, cut four more pieces from ⅜″ diameter or larger cattail stems. They should be 11″ long, and cut with a slant at the bigger end. Arrange stems on table as shown in (B). With smallest diameter of each stem at bottom edge, mark every second or third stem with pencil ½″ in from bottom end.

STEP 2. FORM BASKET: Tie a length of raffia to the smaller wire circle, which will be at the bottom of the basket. Place the first stem, an 11″ one, on the wire circle so that the ½″ mark is on the wire. Tie into position with raffia as shown in (C). Bind the second stem, a 6″ one, into position with the raffia, making sure the ½″ mark is on the wire. Bind in two more 6″ stems, and then one 11″, following the order in which they are laid out on the table (D). Bind all the stems to the wire circle in the same way, and at the last stem, tie the two raffia ends together, but do not cut them off. Stand the basket on the table and make whatever adjustments are necessary to level it.

STEP 3. SET TOP RING: Tie a piece of raffia to the larger wire circle and set it down inside the ring of cattail stems 1½″ from top of basket. Tie the raffia around the nearest stem. Temporarily secure all four handle stems to the top wire circle with picture cord wire, (E). Thread the long raffia end through a large darning needle. Bind all the stems to the top wire circle using the same binding stitch as before; or see (D). except this time loop the raffia one extra time around the wire between each cattail

Fig. 6. *Starting bun basket*

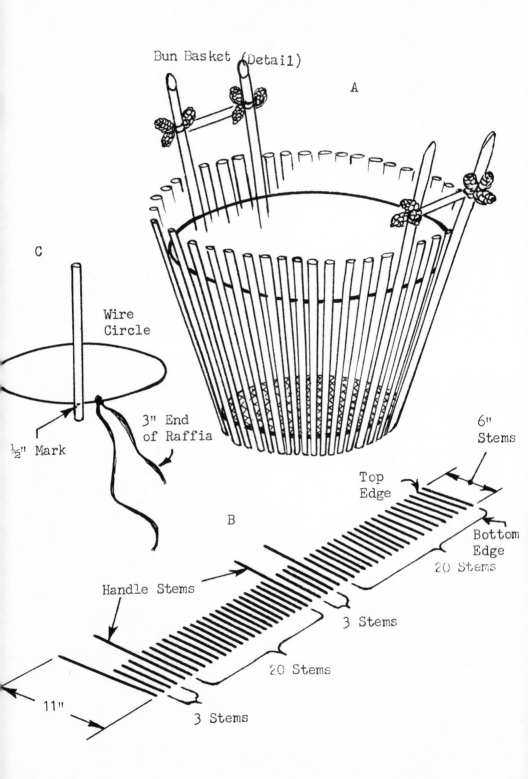

Bun Basket (Detail)

A

C

Wire
Circle

½" Mark

3" End
of Raffia

B

6"
Stems

Top
Edge

Bottom
Edge

20 Stems

Handle Stems

3 Stems

20 Stems

11"

3 Stems

Fig. 7. *Finishing bun basket*

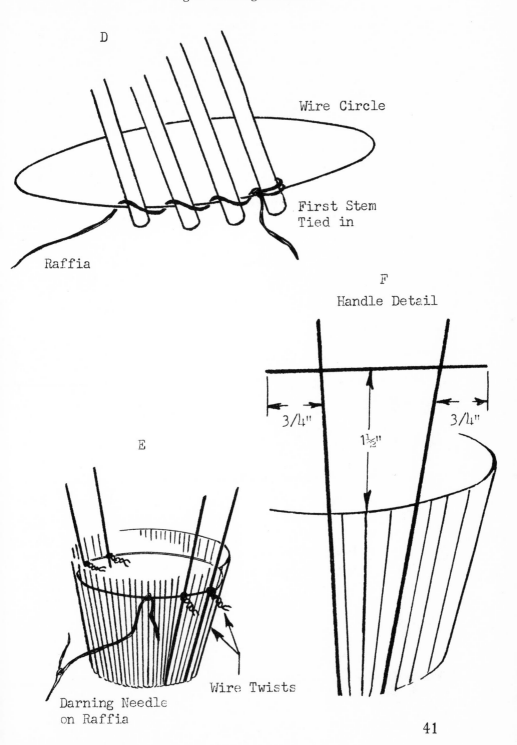

D

Wire Circle

First Stem
Tied in

Raffia

F
Handle Detail

3/4"   1½"   3/4"

E

Wire Twists

Darning Needle
on Raffia

stem — this is primarily to cover wire space left showing between stems. (Note: Stems have a tendency to slant and slide out of position as you are attaching them to the top wire circle. Therefore keep checking and adjusting as you bind this circle into position.) When the stems are all bound to the circle, tie the raffia ends together and cut them off close to the stems.

STEP 4. MAKE BOTTOM, FINISH HANDLES AND ADD ORNAMENTS: The bottom of the basket is woven in, using heavy raffia the same way as jackets for glasses in Fig. 5 (*I*). To complete the handles, cut two pieces of cattail stem long enough to extend about ¾″ on either side of the tall handle stems as shown in Fig. 7, (*F*). Bind these crosspieces with raffia approximately 1½″ above the top of the basket. Ornament with cones, acorns, etc., if desired. Varnish.

MEMO BIRD

This bird will faithfully hold your notes and memos. (See Figs. 8 and 9.)

Materials Needed

> 3 or 4 cattail stems
> Raffia, moistened
> Florists' wire (#12, #18, #26)
> 1 clip clothespin
> Paint, (red and black)

Special Tools

> Needle-nosed pliers with wire cutter on side
> #4 (small, round) paintbrush for painting detail

STEP 1. FEET: Cut two 12″ and four 5″ pieces of cattail stem and soak in warm water. After five minutes, take the 5″ stems out of the water, leaving the other two soaking until needed. At a point 1″ in from the end of each of the four stems, bend them to form an angle. This is done by putting the stem on the table and holding the back edge of a silver knife blade firmly on the 1″ mark. Lift the long end of the stem upward, (*B*). (*Note:* If the stem cracks, don't be concerned, as long as it does not break.) Take the two 12″ stems out of the water and bend each one at two points, once at 5″ and again at 10″, leaving a 2″ end, (*C*). Reinforce these two stems with wire in this way: Cut two 3″ pieces of #12 wire. Straighten out the 2″ bend in the stem and force one 3″ piece of wire all the way into end of stem. This is done by holding stem, as shown in (D), after wire is started, and pushing stem down to force wire up into stem. Do not leave any wire protruding. Rebend wired stem back to its original angle. Reinforce the other stem with wire in the same way. With raffia, bind together the short ends of two of the bent 5″ stems, (E). Repeat with the other two stems. Set one of the bent 12″ stems inside the angle of the bound-together stems as shown in (F). Keeping upright piece pushed tightly back into angle of other piece, pierce holes with a darning needle so that you can push a piece of #18 wire through to hold the two pieces together (G). (Wire should run snugly along outsides of toes and form a "web" between the toes.) Fasten wire firmly by twisting the two ends together with pliers. Clip and turn the end under. Assemble the other foot and leg in the same way. While working on the rest of the bird, place the spurs of the feet under a heavy book, pushing legs into a straight-up-and-down position with the edge of the book (H). Allow to dry in this position.

STEP 2. HEAD: Use a clip clothespin, the closed end of which will form the mouth. Put a length of #18 wire through the eye. Bring ends of wire down on each side and twist together with pliers, close to clothespin underneath (I). Twist for two more inches. (This will be used later to attach head to body.) For the time being, wire clothespin into open position to enable you to paint inside of mouth (J). Paint the inside surface only, as far in toward the clip as possible, using a bright red paint. Use black paint for the spring wire which will be the eye. Put aside to dry; when dry, remove temporary binding wire.

STEP 3. BODY: Cut these pieces of cattail stems with slant ends: Two pieces 1½″ long, four pieces 4″ long and one piece 8″ long (slanted on 1 end only). On the 8″ stem, measure in 3″ from the straight end, and mark. On one 4″ stem, measure in 1″ from one end and mark. This 4″ stem will be his breastbone. Where you just marked these stems, pierce holes with a darning needle. Then pull a #26 fine wire through the holes to bind the two stems together in the position shown in Fig. 9 (K), leaving equal lengths of wire extending on either side of the breastbone. (Both ends of the wire pass through the same hole on the lower stem.) Pull wire snug. At a point 3″ in from the

43

other end of the 8″ stem, put another piece of #26 wire through both stems as before, again leaving equal lengths of wire extending on either side of breastbone (L). Make a hole approximately ¾″ from the end of each of the other cut stems and string them in the order shown in (M), onto the wire extending from the breastbone. (All stems should be strung with the slant facing up.) Pull all the stems close together. Holding the long stem with the attached breastbone in your left hand, wrap the other five stems into a tight cluster around these two in the direction shown in (N). Fasten the two ends of wire by twisting them together tightly with pliers and snipping off close to the body. There should now be an end of wire protruding from each side of the breastbone, (O).

STEP 4. ASSEMBLE: Pierce each leg approximately 1″ from the end on the top angle, remembering to make the hole slightly to one side of the wire reinforcement, (P). Put one leg on each wire as shown in (Q). Pull legs in tight to the body. Pierce each of the three stems that make the top of his back. Draw the wire ends up through these stems to meet on top of back. Fasten ends by twisting tightly with pliers. Snip off and push ends in between two stems. Put one wire stitch through the touching toes to hold the feet secure. Push the twisted wire on the head down into neck, completing the bird, (R).

STEP 5. ADJUSTMENTS: The angle of the body can be adjusted to any position desired, since the top angle of the legs is reinforced with wire inside. If the bend at the ankle needs correction, soak the feet and ankles in hot water and allow to remain standing overnight with spurs under a book as before.

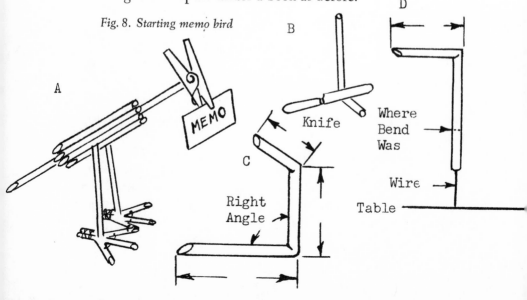

Fig. 8. *Starting memo bird*

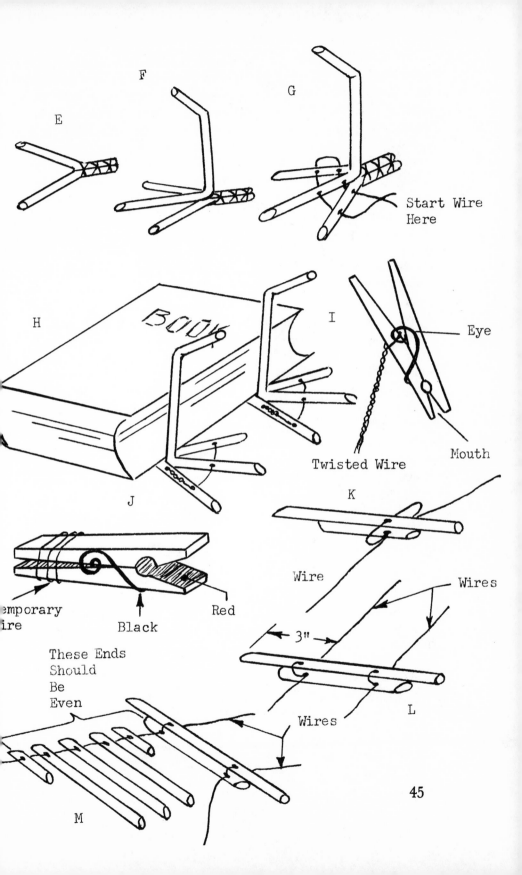

E

F

G

Start Wire
Here

H

BOOK

I

Eye

Twisted Wire

Mouth

J

K

Wire

Temporary
Wire

Black

Red

Wires

3"

Wires

These Ends
Should
Be
Even

Wires

L

M

45

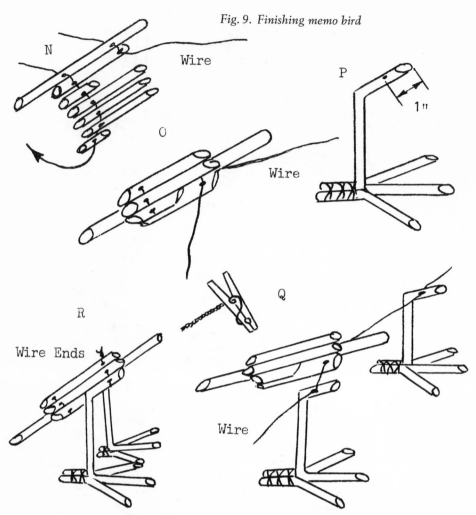

Fig. 9. Finishing memo bird

N

Wire

O

Wire

P

1″

R

Wire Ends

Q

Wire

FLOWERPOT JACKET WITH TRELLIS

Build a flowerpot jacket to beautify any plant container. If the plant needs a trellis, build it into the jacket. This trellis stands 13″ above the pot jacket, which is 6½″ high and 5½″ in diameter. (See Plate 2; Fig. 10.)

Materials Needed

    18 to 20 cattail stems
    Cotton rug yarn, 4 yards long, cut in half (raffia may be used, but isn't
       as durable)
    3 pound shortening can
    Varnish

STEP 1. From small ends and center sections of cattail stems cut 25 pieces 6″ long, 25 pieces 6½″ long; from large ends cut two pieces 19″ long; from small ends cut one piece 14″ long, one piece 16½″ long, and one piece 19″ long.

STEP 2. BUILD JACKET: Stick two thumbtacks into the worktable, 3½″ apart and near the edge. Find the center of both pieces of yarn and put each piece around a tack at the center. Tie a double knot to make a 1″ loop (A). Start with one 6″ stem. Tie this in place with two single knots so that 1″ of stem extends to the right of the yarn. Check to make sure there is a distance of 3½″ on stem between two pieces of yarn, (B). Tie in a 6½″ stem the same way, again leaving one inch at the right, (C). As you build, be careful to alternate large and small ends of each piece. Continue tying in alternate 6″ and 6½″ stems until there are 3″ of tied-together stems. Add a 19″ stem, (D). Use a 6″ stem on either side of the 19″ stem, if possible. Tie in alternate 6″ and 6½″ stems until there are 10″ more of tied-together stems. Tie in the other 19″ stem and continue until there is sufficient length to go around the shortening can, (E). Tie in the last stem with a double knot.

STEP 3. FIT AND VARNISH: Remove thumbtacks; fit jacket around can. Add or remove stems, if necessary, to make it fit. Before tying permanently in place, varnish piece on both sides. At the same time, varnish the three stems to be used as cross-

Plate 2. Flowerpot jacket with trellis

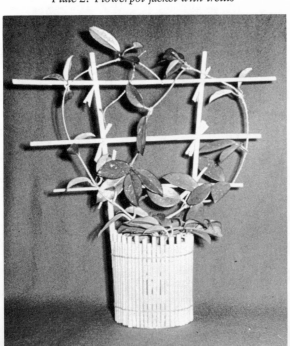

pieces for the trellis. Let dry thoroughly. When dry, tie in place around can. Spread the upright stems slightly apart at the top and tie the 19″ crosspiece 2″ down from the top, leaving 5″ of stem extending on each end. Space the other two stems as shown, (F), completing the trellis.

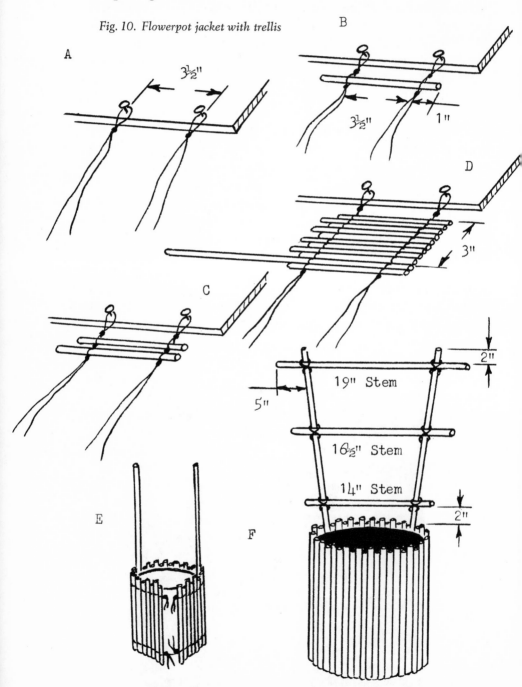

Fig. 10. Flowerpot jacket with trellis

WASTEBASKET

For beauty and utility, try this cattail stem wastebasket which stands 16″ high and is 13″ in diameter. All in natural colors with cones as the decorative focal point, it is indeed a joy to create. (See Figs. 11 and 12.)

Materials Needed

50 cattail stems (approximately)
Raffia, heavy or double strands, moistened
2 heavy wire circles, 12″ in diameter (florists' holly rings)
Screening, 13″ square, brass or copper, for bottom
Picture cord wire
Assorted cones for ornamentation

STEP 1. CUT STEMS:

98 pieces, each 16″ long, use entire stem, ends and centers

4 pieces, each 20″ long, from large ends, for handles

10 pieces, each 8″ long, from small ends, for handles

STEP 2. MAKE BOTTOM: For the bottom you need one of the wire rings and the screening. If you want to give your basket more grace, snip this wire ring where it is joined, overlap the two wire ends about 3″ and wire them together again. The diameter then will be 10½″ or 11″. This slight tapering will make the basket more graceful. From the screening, cut a circle that is ½″ larger all around than the wire ring. Lay the wire ring on the screening, and roll the edge of screening around the ring as best you can, (B). Then use picture cord wire to "sew" the screening to the wire circle all the way around. This is the bottom of the wastebasket.

STEP 3. PUT FRAME TOGETHER: Mark both wire circles exactly at the halfway point, (C), so you will be able to place the handles accurately opposite each other. A good marker is a dab of red nail polish, since it shows up and doesn't rub off. Place a 20″ handle stem on each side of one of the halfway marks on the wire circle which is covered with screening. These must be far enough apart to allow four 16″ stems to go between them, (D) and (E). When you are sure the position will be right, thread a large darning needle with raffia and sew all six items into place using the binding stitch shown in the Jacket for Glass, Fig. 5 (F). You will have to sew through the screening, too. Make sure 1″ of stem extends below wire circle, Fig. 11 (D). Secure raffia

Fig. 11. Starting waste basket

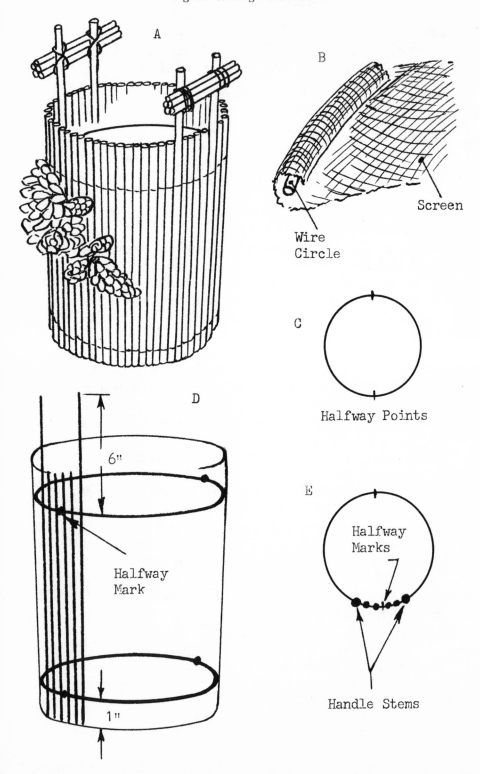

A

B

Screen

Wire
Circle

C

Halfway Points

D

6"

Halfway
Mark

1"

E

Halfway
Marks

Handle Stems

tightly, but do not cut it off. Place the other wire circle 6″ down from the top of the 20″ stems and sew it into place with raffia, (D). Secure raffia again, but do not cut it. Now tightly wire the other two "handle" stems into the correct position on both circles, (F). Do not sew them into position yet, because they may have to be moved to make adjustments later. This should give you a frame to build on, but do not expect it to be at all sturdy yet.

STEP 4. COVER SIDES: As you build the sides, make sure to place the large end of each stem at the top; also, 1″ of stem must extend below the bottom wire circle. On the side where the handle unit has been sewed into place, thread a darning needle with the length of raffia extending from the bottom circle. Bind stems to the lower circle all the way around to the opposite "handle"

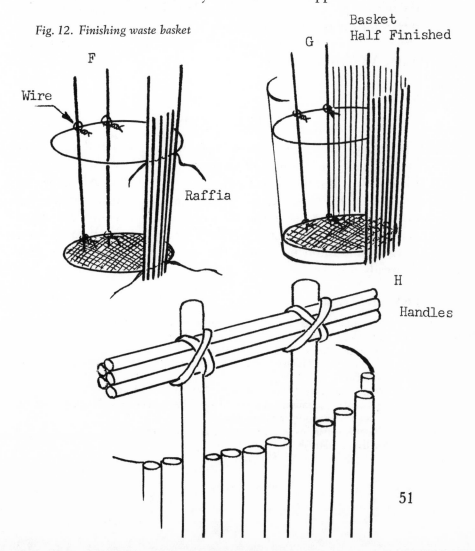

Fig. 12. Finishing waste basket

Basket
Half Finished

F

Wire

G

Raffia

H

Handles

stem and secure the raffia firmly here (G). Now start back at the first handle unit again. Follow the same procedure in binding all the stems to the top wire circle. Keep checking as you go so that each stem stands vertically in position. When half the basket is complete, check once more to see that the handle units are exactly opposite each other. If they are not, make whatever adjustments necessary by moving the one that is only wired in place. When the handles are opposite each other, bind the second set of handles permanently into place, and then continue making the other side of the basket in the same way you did the first side. When all the stems are bound in (top and bottom) tie the raffia ends and snip them off.

STEP 5. FINISH HANDLES AND ADD ORNAMENT: Group together five of the ten 8" pieces that were cut at the beginning and bind them into position as a handle, (H). Use the remaining five pieces for the other handle. Then wire cones, either individually or in a cluster, to the basket to form the design or pattern you want. Varnish or shellac.

DOLL   HOUSE

The house pictured is a good-sized doll house, a full yard long by 18" wide, and stands 19" high at the peak of the roof. (See Plates 3-6; Figs. 13-15.) To make it, you will need plenty of straight, large cattail stems. To insure an adequate supply for many cattail projects, I usually gather at least a hundred stems per year in late October, store them in an unheated garage, and leave them untouched until the following spring when they are ready for use.

Materials Needed

> 300 cattail stems (more or less, since length of stem varies in different locales), for complete house and furniture
> Raffia, moistened
> Molding for windows and doors, (about 13' to 14' of ¾" rounded edge or flat)
> Heavy cardboard (from corrugated boxes) for roof and peaks
> Long, heavy straight pins 2¼" long (dressmaker pins are okay, but are not as strong) for holding roof
> 10' lattice strip ½" x 1½", for roof reinforcement
> Shellac or varnish

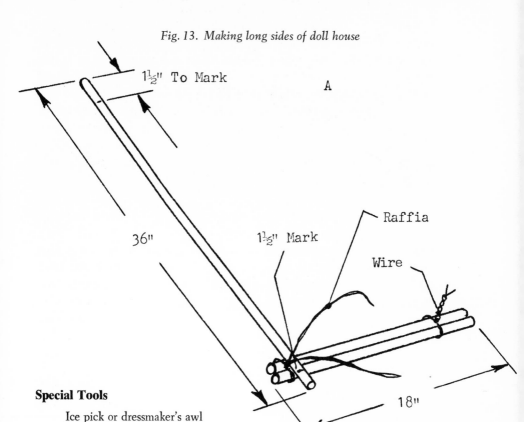

Fig. 13. Making long sides of doll house

1½" To Mark   A

Raffia

36"   1½" Mark   Wire

Special Tools

Ice pick or dressmaker's awl
Small fine-toothed saw

18"

STEP 1. PLAN HOUSE: In planning the house, it is wise to scale it to some specific figure, such as 1″ to the foot to insure that all parts will fit and look well together. Then keep to that scale through the entire project. *Draw your plans on paper first.* Draw each side to scale showing windows and doors exactly as you want them. Consider where partitions for rooms will be inside the house to determine where you need windows or doors. Each side of the house will be made separately, as a flat piece, like the Serving Tray in Plate 1, Figs. 2 and 3. It will be a large, flat mat first, with all the cattail stems bound with raffia to several supporting stems in back. Then windows and doors will be cut out and edged with molding. As you consider placement of windows and doors, remember that each side must have several of these supporting stems inside, and you must arrange your openings so that it will not be necessary to cut through any of the supporting stems.

53

Plate 3. Doll house front and patio

STEP 2. MAKE LONG SIDES: Build the longest walls first. This allows you to select the longest and strongest stems to use here where they are needed. For each side, select 44 or 45 long, strong stems, enough to build a wall 16″ high, and cut 36″ from the larger ends. Cut six more pieces 18″ long from the center sections of stems for vertical supports. Save all small ends; any that are 12″ long can be used later for the roof and shorter ones for furniture. These vertical supports, or uprights, are about 2″ longer than the finished height of the wall. This extra 2″ is left at the bottom of the wall, making 2″ dowels that push down into a styrofoam base when you want to stand the wall in place.

Before starting to build, measure 1½″ in from each end of the 36″ pieces, and mark with a pencil. These marks serve as a guide for keeping the uprights laced squarely to the long stems, and as you lace, the raffia will hide the marks. To build the wall, you will start binding long stems onto the uprights from the top and work down. Temporarily wire two of the 18″ uprights together, tie a long piece of raffia around the end of these pieces, and set one 36″ stem across it as shown in (A). (You will need about two yards of raffia here, and if you wet it before using, it will be more pliable.) Use the same binding stitch with raffia as shown in (C) and (D). Be sure to fasten this first long stem firmly, and as near the top of the uprights as possible. Set another 36″ stem in place at the 1½″ mark, and bind it into position the same way. Continue placing 36″ stems and binding them until you have 16″ of stems bound to the uprights.

Alternate the thick ends of the cattails so that your walls are the same height at each side. It will help to measure your work

54

as you go along, so that you can place a thick or thin end where it is needed to make both sides equal. If you complete a 16″ height of wall before you have used 44 stems, just stop adding stems and fasten the raffia securely. Anchor or clamp your work to some heavy object if possible; this will make the placing and tying of stems much easier. (*See Flower Pot Jacket.*) You now have one pair of uprights bound in position on one end of the wall.

This first wall is the long wall which will have only a single opening — the door. The placement of doors and windows will determine to some extent the position of the uprights, but this wall gives no problem; the two remaining uprights are placed symmetrically, one in the center, the other on the end. Temporarily wire two more 18″ uprights together and tie raffia on the end as before. Set this pair of uprights halfway down the length of the 36″ stems and bind it in place as you did the first one. When you need one or two uprights between the ends, bind them in sequence as you work across the wall; if the two outside ends are done first, it's more difficult to bind in the middle rows. Bind the third pair of uprights to the other end, and this completes the first wall.

Make the second long wall exactly the same as the first, with the exception of the placement of the upright supports. Consider what openings you will have, and determine position of uprights with an eye for balance and good design. Our house has three windows in this wall making four uprights necessary.

Plate 4. Doll house rear view

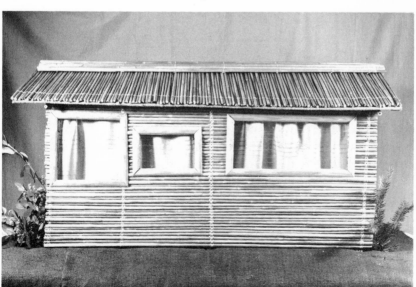

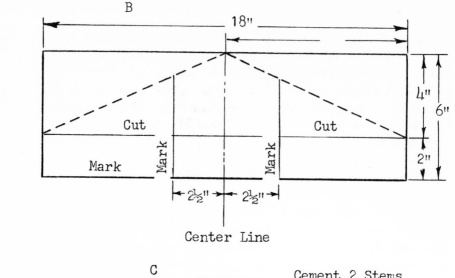

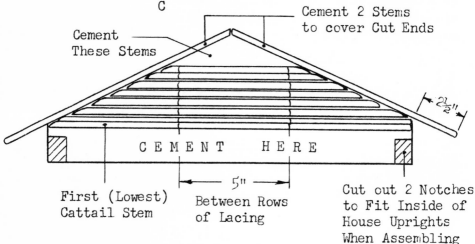

Fig. 14. *Making doll house roof peak*

STEP 3. MAKE SHORT SIDES: Both short sides are made in two pieces; a rectangular piece 18″ long x 16″ high, and a triangular peak.

Rectangular piece: For the rectangular part of each side, cut the following cattail stems: 40 to 45 pieces, 18″ long (from large ends), for siding; 6 pieces, 18″ long (from center section), for uprights. Make this part of both short sides exactly as you did the long sides, considering where openings will be and spacing uprights accordingly.

Peak: Using two pieces of heavy cardboard 6″ x 18″, cut each backing for the peak as shown in (B). Mark three lines on each piece as in (B). One 2″ up from bottom, for placement of first cattail stem, and two for a lacing guide 2½″ on each side of center line. Thread raffia into a heavy darning needle, and, punching holes in the cardboard with an awl or ice pick as you need them, set an 18″ stem across on the line 2″ up from the bottom and lace it to the cardboard at one of the lacing guidelines. Set another shorter stem just above this one and lace it, too, to the cardboard. Work up toward the peak, making each stem shorter than the one before. At the peak, fasten the raffia securely; then lace each stem on the second guide line. There will be a small area above the laced stems where three or four stems will have to be cemented onto the cardboard instead of being laced in place. When the cement is dry, cut these stems to the proper angle.

Assemble peak to rectangular part of side: You will have a 2″ width of cardboard extending below the longest laced-on cattail stem. Lay the rectangular part of the wall on top of this cardboard flap so that the cattail stems on both pieces join properly; then measure and cut out the necessary notches for the uprights that are in the way. See (C). Finally, cement the two pieces together and let dry. Cut two good-sized cattail stems so that they will extend 2½″ beyond the wall as a roof overhang (C). Cement them in place to cover the cut ends of the stems in the peak.

STEP 4. SHELLAC: When all four wall sections are completed, give them a coat of clear, white shellac, being careful to apply it thickly on all cut ends. Shellac one side and let dry; then turn it over and shellac the other side. I usually cover the inside (that with the uprights) first, and do the outside last.

STEP 5. CUT DOORS AND WINDOWS: At this point you may cut out the windows and doors. Use a straightedge to mark across the stems so you will have a nice straight-sided window. You can cut the stems with a razor blade, linoleum knife or a small hobby saw. If the top and bottom stems are not quite straight, the molding trim will cover them. Shellac all cut ends and let dry.

For a window approximately 7″ x 7″, you will need 34″ to 36″ of ¾″ molding. Measure each side of the opening carefully so you don't come out short; then cut each piece to a 45° angle at each end. When the four pieces have been properly fitted to the opening, cement them in place. Try to keep the joints close together. The molding may be held in place with clamps, or the whole section laid flat and weights placed to hold the molding until dry.

Doorways are made in the same way, except that there will be no molding on the bottom side. Make the door itself from heavy cardboard shellacked on both sides; brass paper fasteners make excellent door knobs. Attach clear plastic inside window openings to give appearance of glass.

Step 6. base: The house must be mounted on some sort of base before the roof can be made. I used three sheets of 2" thick styrofoam 12" x 36". The 2" extension of the uprights at the bottom of each side can easily be pushed down into the styrofoam to make each section stand. Place the long sides first, and when placing the end sections, arrange them so that the 2½" roof overhang comes down and over the top of the long side, helping to hold all four sides close together.

Step 7. roof: The roof backing is also heavy cardboard. Measure for size of roof: For *length*, measure length of house and add at least 2" on each end for eaves; for *width*, measure from peak on end section down to tip of overhanging stem, and double it. On our house the roof measurement is 40" long and 25" wide. Cut a piece of heavy corrugated cardboard to the required size, score and crease it down its length *exactly* in the center. Shellac the inside and let dry; then do the outside and allow it to dry with the sides at a slight angle. This is the roof foundation.

To keep the roof flat, since the cardboard may have a tendency to sag, reinforce it with four flat strips of ½" thick wood, 1½" wide by about 32" long, (D). Cement the strips in place well in from all edges so that they will not interfere when placing roof on house.

The roof may be used as is, or the outer surface may be covered with burlap or other textured material. The house pictured has a cattail roof which is made as follows: Cut enough pieces from the small ends of cattail stems to cover one side of roof — 136 pieces, 13" long. Using the method described for the Flowerpot Jacket, lace together a mat 40" long x 13" wide, keeping the rows of lacing about 2" in from each end. Repeat procedure to

Fig. 15. Reinforcing the roof   D

Inside of Roof

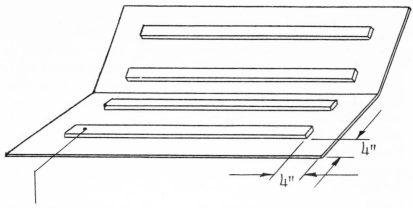

Wood Strips
½" thick x 1½" wide

make mat for other side of roof. Lay these mats flat and straight, and shellac them on one side. Let dry and do other side. When both mats are dry, lay them in position on the roof, and tie or lace them together at the peak. To cover the lacing, make a ridge pole by lacing together about 16 stems each 40″ long. Four rows of lacing will be enough. Shellac and let dry.

STEP 8. PATIO: The patio is placed on the long side of the house with the door. It consists of six large stems as supporting columns for the stem-covered 10″ x 20″ cardboard roof. For the supporting columns, cut two pieces 10½″ long and four pieces 12″ long.

Plate 5. Doll house right end view

Lace the two 10½″ stems to the side of the house, one just inside the lacings at the corner, and the other 16″ to the right of it, just beyond the door. See Plate 3. Push the four 12″ pieces down into the styrofoam as outer corner supports. It may be better to wait until the roof is ready before placing these four supports.

Shellac the roof cardboard, first one side and let dry, then the other. While it is drying, cut from small or medium ends of cattail stems about 30 pieces 21″ long. Lace these stems together with raffia to make a 10″ x 21″ mat or roof cover. Sew this mat with raffia to the cardboard roof, or cement it in place if you prefer. Set the patio roof in position over the two supporting columns which are attached to the side of the house, and hold it in place by pushing a long pin (corsage pins will do) down through the roof into the top of each column. Set the other four columns in good position, push them down into the styrofoam base, and secure the roof to them, too, with long pins. This completes the outside of the house.

STEP 9. PARTITIONS: You have doubtless noticed that each section of the house is complete in itself and can be set up quickly and easily; or stored in a minimum of space. If you wish to furnish the house, divide the area into rooms. If a cardboard or plywood second oor is desired, attach long stems inside halfway up each wall, on which it can rest. Then both the upstairs and the downstairs can be divided into two good-sized rooms by using a plywood or cardboard partition in each. And for easy access to all four rooms, just remove one of the long outer walls!

Plate 6. Doll house left end view

MINIATURE FURNITURE

Cattail timber offers endless possibilities for creating all kinds of furniture for the youngsters. With a little help, even an eight-year-old can make this miniature furniture. The four rooms following are made in proportion to the cattail house. Instructions are given for making furniture, all 3″ to 5″ high, and drapes, rugs, wallpaper, etc. offer an opportunity to try your hand at interior decoration.

Materials Needed

Cattail stems (see Note)
small diameter, 3/16″ to 1/4″
medium diameter, 5/16″ to 3/8″
large diameter, 7/16″ to 1/2″
Raffia, moistened
Straight pins
Balsa wood (comes in standard sizes, but may measure a trifle short; allowance for this is made in directions).
Lightweight cardboard (such as found in men's shirts or hosiery), for support frames
Brass paper fasteners, for knobs
Cement
Shellac or varnish

Note: If large diameter stems are split down through the middle, it will take fewer stems than if small diameter stems are used. Split stems may be used cut side down or cut side out. Both ways are effective. Sometimes using each side out alternately will give the effect wanted.

DINING ROOM

A table and six chairs, a buffet and a hutch, all made of cattail stems, are the furnishings of this quite elegant dining room. Seats and backs of chairs are woven raffia, while flat surfaces on table, buffet and hutch are balsa wood.

A soft robin's egg blue wallpaper with white figures covers the walls, and the drapes add a darker value of the same color. The rug is tweed, using light and dark shades of the same blue. Miniature antique dishes serve as accessories to complete the picture. (See Plates 7 and 8; Figs. 16-18.)

The technique for making all the miniature furniture is essentially the same. The most important thing to remember

Plate 7. Rocking chair and dining room furniture

is to measure and cut the cattail stems accurately. The smaller the piece you are working with, the more accuracy required.

Chair

STEP 1. Cut the following pieces from small or middle sections of cattail stems: 2 pieces 3½″ long and 11 pieces 1¾″ long. Place two short stems perpendicular to each other, (B), and fasten together by carefully pushing a straight pin all the way down into the stem. Add two more short stems to make unit (C) which will be the chair front.

STEP 2. With pencil, mark the two 3½″ stems halfway, at 1¾″. Make two units using one long and two short stems for chair sides, (D). The measurements of these two units must correspond exactly with the first unit. Join the two sides to the front (E), and to complete frame, insert three rungs missing from the back.

STEP 3. At this point, level chair and make any adjustments necessary for it to stand straight and firm. Then, to strengthen it, carefully pull one pin at a time partially out, place a drop of cement in the joint, and replace the pin. Do this for each joint and let chair dry. For me, this method of cementing joints after the piece is together has produced straighter and stronger furniture than when each joint is glued as it is initially put together.

STEP 4. To weave seat, thread darning needle with a long piece of raffia and tie other end to back corner of chair seat. Twist raffia into a cord and start working from back to front over and under seat rungs until it crosses about ten times. Then bring raffia under front corner and out to the side, (F). Now start weaving across top of seat to other side, and, to come back to this side, pass raffia under seat without weaving it in, (G). Continue till seat is woven, and finish it at same corner where raffia was tied at start. Tie the two ends of raffia together, snip off and tuck under. Shellac or varnish.

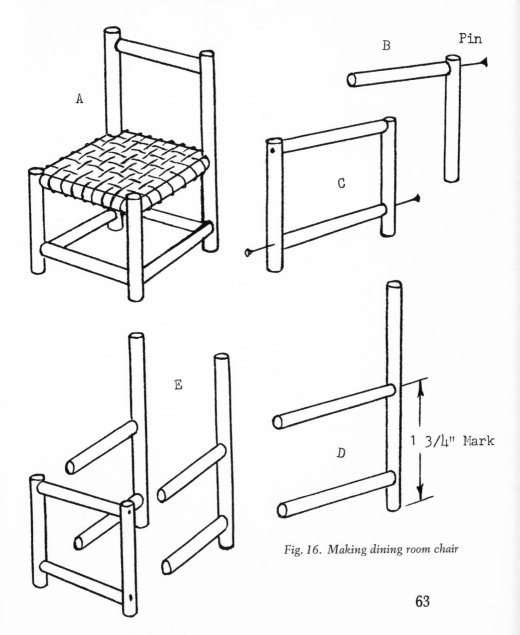

Fig. 16. Making dining room chair

Fig. 17. Weaving chair seat

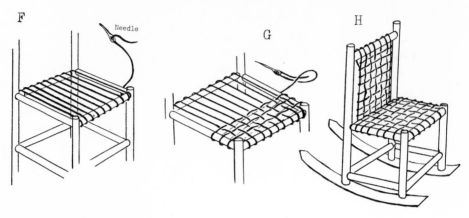

Rocking Chair

Make chair as above and then pin and glue rockers in place; make rockers by cutting and shaping them from a strip of splint, (H).

Table

Cut a piece of balsa wood the size you wish for the top. Then cut four pieces of cattail stems for legs and two for cross braces. Reinforce the cross braces by pushing a piece of #18 wire into each one for its full length. This wire reinforcement makes it possible to bend the braces as in (I) and (J). Put the legs and cross braces together first with pins and cement and level them carefully. Put a drop of cement on top of each table leg, set the balsa top in position, and press a pin down through it into the leg underneath. To strengthen the under support, wrap the cross braces with raffia where they meet.

Fig. 18. Making dining room table

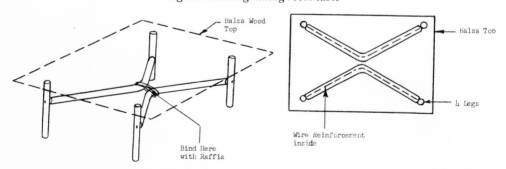

Plate 8. Dining room: hutch, chairs, table and buffet

Hutch and Buffet

For both the hutch and the buffet, use same basic method as for chest of drawers in the master bedroom, See Fig. 20 (B).

MASTER BEDROOM

The master bedroom has a king-size bed, two nightstands, each with a lamp; a dresser, a chest of drawers, an armchair and a floor lamp. The lamps are all made with cattail stems on balsa wood bases, and luffa sponge slices for shades. Colors of the drapes and bedspread are light to dark values of peacock blue and orchid on white in a modern swirl design. The rug is the darkest value of blue, and the walls are painted the lightest blue. (Plates 9-12; Figs. 19-22.)

King Size Bed

STEP 1. From the large ends of cattail stems cut the following pieces:

    2 pieces, 7½" long, for head and foot rails
    2 pieces, 6½" long, for side rails
    4 pieces, 3½" long, for head legs
    4 pieces, 2" long, for foot legs
    4 pieces, 3½" long, for crosspieces at head and foot
    2 pieces, 2¾" long and 2 pieces, 2" long, for headboard decorations

65

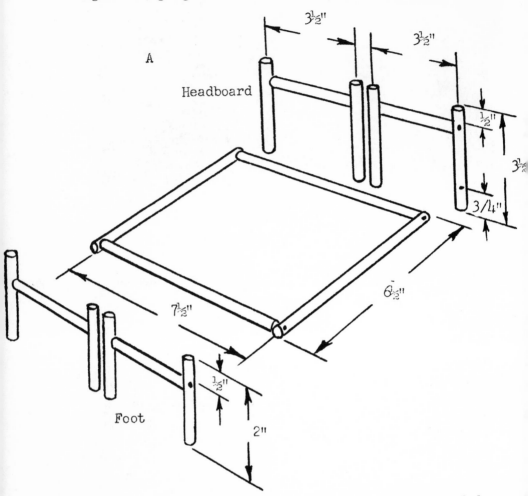

Fig. 19. Making king size bed

A

Headboard

$3\frac{1}{2}''$

$3\frac{1}{2}''$

$\frac{1}{2}''$

$3\frac{1}{2}''$

$3/4''$

$6\frac{1}{2}''$

$7\frac{1}{2}''$

$\frac{1}{2}''$

Foot

$2''$

Step 2. Make a rectangular frame using the two 7½″ and the two 6½″ stems. Cement and pin together. Make the headboard section using four 3½″ stems for legs and two 3½″ crosspieces. Make the foot of the bed with four 2″ legs and two 3½″ crosspieces, (A).

Step 3. Attach head and foot of bed to the 7½″ sides of the frame so that all the legs are ¾″ long from the frame to the floor. Cement and pin the remaining four cut pieces into place as headboard decorations, and finally, cement a ⅜″-thick piece of balsa wood 6¾″ x 8″ to the frame for the box spring. Shellac or varnish.

Plate 9. *King size bed and twin bed*

Chest of Drawers

To make the chest of drawers and the dresser in master bedroom, or the buffet and the hutch in dining room, follow this method: First, you need a cardboard frame slightly smaller than the finished piece will be. After the frame is made, cattail stems are laced or cemented to it, balsa wood tops put on and knobs added.

STEP 1. Make the cardboard frame for the chest of drawers as shown in (B).

STEP 2. From center sections of cattail stems cut 27 pieces 5″ long, for back and sides; from large sections cut 10 pieces 5″ long and from small sections cut 5 pieces 4½″ long, for front. Lace together all 27 of the 5″ center-section pieces with raffia. This should make a strip of stems 5″ wide by approximately 8″ long. Cement this strip to the sides and back of the cardboard frame.

STEP 3. Now cement stems to the front to achieve desired effect. For the chest of drawers, split the ten large-diameter 5″ pieces and use them flat side out to give the effect of drawers. Start by cementing one 4½″ small-diameter stem across the front at top of frame. Then cement two of the 5″ split stems immediately below it, flat side out. Continue, cementing one small, round and two large, flat stems to the bottom of the frame.

Fig. 20. *Chest of drawers pattern*

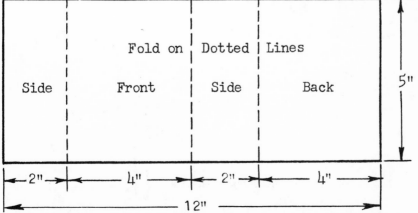

Plate 10. *Master bedroom chest of drawers and dresser*

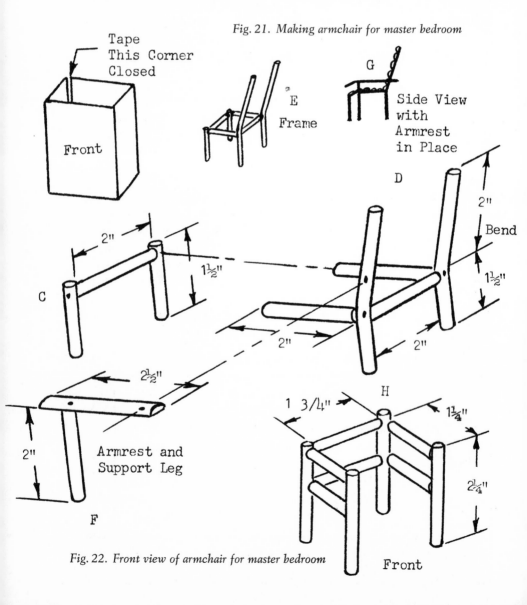

Fig. 21. *Making armchair for master bedroom*

Tape
This Corner
Closed

Front

E
Frame

G

Side View
with
Armrest
in Place

D

2"

Bend

1½"

C

2"

1½"

2"

2"

2½"

2"

Armrest and
Support Leg

F

H

1 3/4"

1¼"

2¼"

Fig. 22. *Front view of armchair for master bedroom*

Front

STEP 4. Cement on a ⅜″ thick of balsa wood, 5 ¾″ x 3″, for the top. When all cement is dry, push paper fasteners through front for drawer pulls, letting them extend in front of stems just a little (about 3/16″), as real knobs would. Shellac or varnish.

Armchair

STEP 1. Cut the following pieces of cattail stems: two pieces 3½″ long, for back and legs; two pieces 1½″ long, for front legs; four pieces 2″ long, for crosspieces (front to back and side to side); two pieces 2″ long, for armrest legs; two pieces 2½″ long, for armrest; 12 to 17 pieces 3¼″ long, for seat and back. These pieces for the seat and back may be cut from large-diameter stems and split down through the middle if desired; this will require fewer stems than using whole, small-diameter pieces.

STEP 2. Make front legs unit, (C). Before making unit for back of chair, (D), reinforce the two 3½″ back pieces with a piece of #18 wire up through the middle of each piece. Measure up 1½″ and bend the stems gently to a slight angle. This will give a slanting back. Place the three seat crosspieces just under this bend. Add front legs unit to complete frame, (E).

STEP 3. With raffia, lace all the 3¼″ seat and back pieces onto the frame using method described in making Serving Tray (Fig. 2). A large darning needle threaded on each end of the raffia may be helpful.

STEP 4. Make two armrest units with supporting leg, Fig. 21, (F), and attach to chair as in (G).

End Tables

STEP 1. Cut the following pieces of cattail stems: four pieces 2¼″ long, for legs; four pieces 1¼″ long, for side crosspieces; two pieces 1¾″ long, for back crosspieces; one piece 2½″ long, large-diameter stem split in half, for front crosspiece.

STEP 2. Make table frame as shown in (H). Then set the 2½″ split stem in place across the front. Level the legs carefully and place a drop of cement to top of each leg. Lay a ⅜″-thick piece of balsa wood 2″ x 2½″ on top and press a pin down through each leg. Weight the top and let dry. Shellac or varnish.

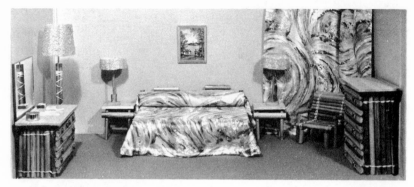

Plate 11. Master bedroom: dresser, floor lamp, end tables with lamps, bed, armchair and chest of drawers

Table Lamps

Step 1. Cut a 1″ square from ⅜″-thick balsa wood for a base. From a ½″ diameter cattail stem, cut a half-inch long piece and cement it in the center of the balsa base.

Step 2. Cut a 2″ long piece of a small diameter (¼″) cattail stem. This must be small enough to be forced down into the ½″ diameter stem, telescope fashion, and cemented. Tape a 1½″ piece of #22 wire, push it down into the top of the small cattail stem, and cement it there. Leave enough wire extending from the top to hold the lampshade. Shellac.

Step 3. Make lampshade from a ⅞″-thick slice of luffa sponge (see chapter III Plate 18), 2″ to 2¼″ in diameter, with the inner membranes left intact, and push shade down on wire.

Plate 12. Living room pole lamp; bedroom floor and table lamps

Floor Lamp

STEP 1. From ⅜"-thick balsa wood, cut two squares, one 1¾", the other 1¼". Cut or round-off corners, as desired, and cement squares together as shown in Plate 12.

STEP 2. Cut three cattail stems (⅜" diameter) 5½" long for the upright part of the lamp. With raffia, lace them together from top to bottom and fasten ends securely. Cement this upright in the exact center of the balsa wood base.

STEP 3. For shade holder, wrap three 3½"-long pieces of #22 wire individually with Floratape, then wrap together for 2". Cement the wrapped end into the center of the three cattail stems. About ½" to ¾" from the top, bend the ends out at right angles to hold the shade. When all cement is dry, shellac lamp.

STEP 4. For shade, cut a 2"-long slice from a 2½"-diameter luffa sponge. Cut all the membranes out of the sponge except for a ¾" thickness at the top. This will rest on the wires and hold the shade in place.

LIVING ROOM

The living room is done in white, gold, black and teal blue. The black fireplace in the rear is made from two blocks of wood — one piece 2" square and 20" long is the base, and the other, a 12" long piece of 2" x 4" with a half circle cut out, becomes the fireplace. Fairy driftwood, a small oriental figurine and a play watch for a clock decorate the mantel and the space above it. Two ceramic cats and two crocheted round cushions are of robin's egg blue, and the wallpaper is a tint of the same blue with white figures. Curtains are white with gold stripe nylon, and the rug is white fur cloth. Shell ashtrays and a Holy Bible only 1" x 1½" catch the eye on the coffee table.

Plate 13. Two views of armchair

The furniture has all been painted white to carry out the color scheme. It consists of a davenport, two armchairs, a coffee table, two end tables with lamps on each, and a floor lamp. (See Plates 12-15; Fig. 23.)

Armchair

STEP 1. Make cardboard frame, see pattern, Fig. 23 (A). Using staples, cement or tape, fasten the cardboard frame together as in (B). Then bring two wings forward and fasten, to hold back of frame at proper angle.

STEP 2. Using large-diameter cattail stems, split in half so they will lay flat, cut 13 pieces, 3" long. Cement these stems to cover the apron, seat, and back rest of the chair.

STEP 3. From medium- or small-diameter stems, cut 12 pieces 1½" long for armrests, and 19 pieces 3¼" long for wings and back. Lace six of the 1½" stems together with raffia (see *Armchair, Master Bedroom* Fig. 21.) Continue lacing, adding the 3¼" stems one at a time, and finish the mat with the six remaining 1½" stems. Measure as you add stems so that the finished mat will fit perfectly around sides and back of cardboard frame.

STEP 4. Cement this mat to the frame, and when dry, shellac or paint.

Davenport

Materials Needed

> 12 pieces, 2" long, for arms
> 30 pieces, 3" long, for wings and back
> 13 pieces, 7" long large-diameter stems (split), for apron, seat and back
> 2 pieces, 2" long and 2 pieces, 1¾" long and 2 pieces 1½" long, for inside of arms

Plate 14. Living room: Two arm chairs with tables and lamps, fireplace, coffee table, pole lamp and davenport

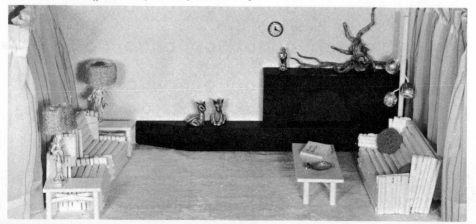

Plate 15. Living room davenport and armchair

The davenport is made in the same way as the armchair. The distance between the arms is increased from 3″ to 7″ and an armrest has been added inside the arms. Also, after the stems on the seat have been cemented in place, they are hand-stitched to the frame for additional strength and decorative interest.

Coffee Table

The coffee table is made the same as the dining room table, i.e., the legs and cross braces are put together and leveled first, then the balsa wood top is cemented and pinned in place.

Materials Needed

    4 pieces cattail stems, 1½″ long, for legs
    2 pieces stems, 5″ long, for crosspieces under table
    Balsa wood, ⅜″ thick, 6″ x 2½″, for table top
    2 pieces #18 wire, 5″ long, for crosspiece reinforcement
    Pins, shellac, cement, raffia

Side Tables

Same as coffee table except for size.

Materials Needed

    4 pieces, 1¾″ long, for legs
    2 pieces, ¾″ long, for end crosspiece
    2 pieces, 2½″ long, for crosspieces under table
    2 pieces #18 wire, 2½″ long, for crosspiece reinforcement
    Balsa wood (⅜″ thick), 1½″ x 3″, for table top

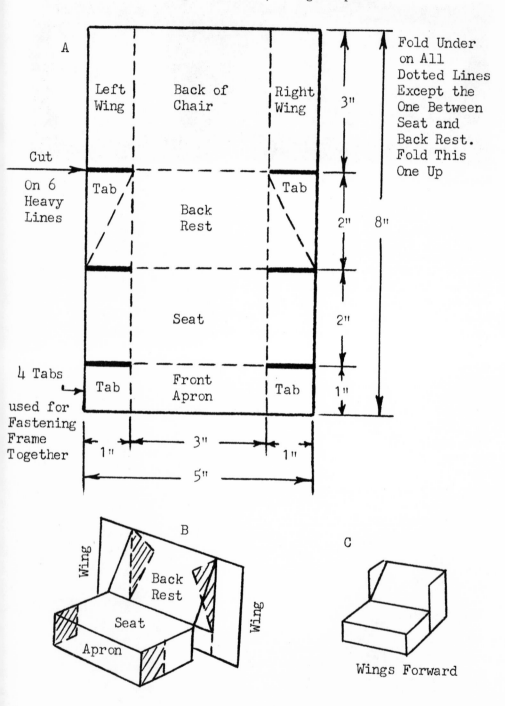

Fig. 23. *Armchair for living room pattern*

A

Left Wing

Back of Chair

Right Wing

3"

Fold Under on All Dotted Lines Except the One Between Seat and Back Rest. Fold This One Up

Cut

On 6 Heavy Lines

Tab

Back Rest

Tab

2"

8"

4 Tabs

used for Fastening Frame Together

Tab

Front Apron

Tab

Seat

2"

1"

1"

3"

1"

5"

B

Wing

Back Rest

Wing

Seat

Apron

C

Wings Forward

Lamps for Side Tables

These lamps are made from a pair of miniature oriental figurines about 3″ high. Three taped wires, taped together for the greater length, run up the back of the figure and are bent out at right angles about one inch from the top. This provides support for the luffa sponge shade. (Plate 14.)

Pole Lamp

Materials Needed

>1 piece wood, ⅝″ thick and 1½″ square, for base
>1 cattail stem, medium diameter, 8″ long, for pole
>3 acorn cups, for lights
>3 pieces #22 wire, about 1″ long, to hold lights
>1 piece #22 wire, about 2″ long, to hold pole

STEP 1. Wrap all four pieces of wire with Floratape. Drill a hole in the center of the wood base and cement the 2″ long wire in it. Put some cement on the end of the cattail stem and push it down onto the other end of the wire until the stem rests firmly on the base. Let cement dry.

STEP 2. Drill holes in the center of the tip ends of the acorns, cement the 1″ wires into the holes and let dry.

STEP 3. Drill three holes at a downward angle on the pole where the lights are to be placed. The first light is 4″ high, the second is 1″ higher on the opposite side of the pole, and the third is another inch up but on the same side of the pole as the first. Cement the three acorn-light wires into these holes and let dry. Paint white with gold acorns and base.

3. CHARACTER DOLLS

Making character dolls can be a delightful hobby. Costs can be kept to a minimum by using discards and natural materials. To me, the best dolls by far are those made with a wire frame or armature. (Figs. 24-25.)

ARMATURE FOR A NINE-INCH DOLL

Materials Needed

> 1 medium-size pecan nut, for head
> 2 pieces, 18" long, #22 wire for neck and shoulders
> 2 pieces, 18" long, #24 wire for hands
> 3 pieces, 18" long, #18 wire for body
> 1 piece, 18" long, #18 wire for feet
> Brown Floratape
> Hobby cement

STEP 1. HEAD: Since the size of the body frame depends upon the head (the figure should be roughly seven heads high), first decide which sort of head you will make. The head may be anything from nuts (pecans, walnuts, Brazil nuts) to eggshells, apples, dried lemons or oranges to cornhusks or styrofoam balls. For this basic figure, a pecan nut head was used. *To make a nut head,* drill a hole about ½" deep in the rounded end of the pecan. Drill two more holes for eyes and one for mouth. If this character is going to wear a hat, make a flat place on top of the nut by cutting off about ¼". Snip four pieces of #22 wire about 6" long. Wrap each wire individually with Floratape and then join by wrapping them together with tape for about one inch at one end (this is the neck). Place a generous bit of cement on this end and push it into the hole in the nut. Set aside to dry (A).

STEP 2. HANDS: Hands for dolls are all made in the same manner, but care should be taken to have them in good proportion to the rest of the body. For proper size relationship, follow this guide: The length of the hand from the tip of the middle finger to the wrist will be approximately the same length as the head is from chin to hairline.

Wrap an 18" length of #24 wire with Floratape. Make the wrapping smooth and tight. Now cut five pieces about 2¼" long from this taped wire. Place four of these lengths side by side, adjusting them to conform to the proportions of your own fingers (middle finger is longest and little finger is shortest). Tape these four wires together about ¾″ down from tip of middle finger — twice around with the tape will do (B).

Now take the fifth piece of wire and make it thicker by wrapping two more thicknesses of tape on it for about an inch on one end. This is the thumb and should be larger around than the fingers. Place it in position next to and about ⅜″ shorter than the forefinger. The tip of the thumb comes slightly higher than the point where the fingers join the hand. Study your own hand for the natural length and position of thumb and fingers in relation to each other. About ¾″ down from tip of the thumb, start taping all together, and continue for the length of the wires. All wires should lay side by side — flat and not bunched on top of each other (C). This makes one hand. Make the second hand the same way as the first and lay aside. When the doll is finished, the fingers are bent into the desired position with pliers.

Step 3. Body Frame: Take three pieces of #18 wire (each 18″ long) and wrap separately with Floratape. This taping helps to hold the wires in place as you work with them, since the tape acts as a bond and sticks to itself. Tape the three wires together. Now bend this 18″ wire into a flattened hairpin shape. The flattened section, or shoulders, should be from 1½″ to 2″ across depending on whether it will be a female or male figure. Measure 7½″ down from shoulders and bend the end of the wire forward as part of the foot. (D). Cross the wires to make the waist (3″ to 3½″ down from shoulders) and wrap securely with tape (E).

Step 4. Arms: For arms, tape one 12″ length of #18 wire. Center it across shoulders and wrap securely with tape (F).

Step 5. Feet: Cut two 6″ lengths of #18 wire. Wrap each one with tape. Turn up 2″ at each end of both wires, and bring both ends of the wire together forming a loop between (G). Then tape these feet to the bottoms of the leg wires (H).

Step 6. assemble: head to body. Spread the wires coming from the nut head into 2 strands and bend at right angles about ½″ down from nut. Center the neck on the shoulders and tape the wires together down the length of the arm wires (I).

hands to arms. (Fig. 25). Bend arms down. The hand, when down at the side, is about two-thirds of the distance between the waist and knee. Cut wires, if necessary, to achieve this proportion. The arms will be about 3½″ long. Tape hands into position (J). Care should be taken to place the hands with the thumbs up and at the same level on both sides.

Fig. 24. *Starting armature for nine inch doll*

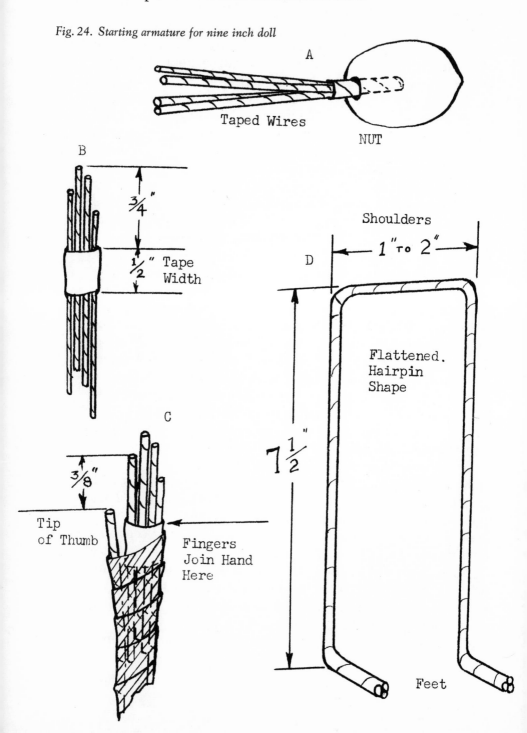

A

Taped Wires

NUT

B

¾″

½″ Tape
Width

C

⅜″

Tip
of Thumb

Fingers
Join Hand
Here

Shoulders

D   1″ ᴛᴏ 2″

Flattened.
Hairpin
Shape

7½″

Feet

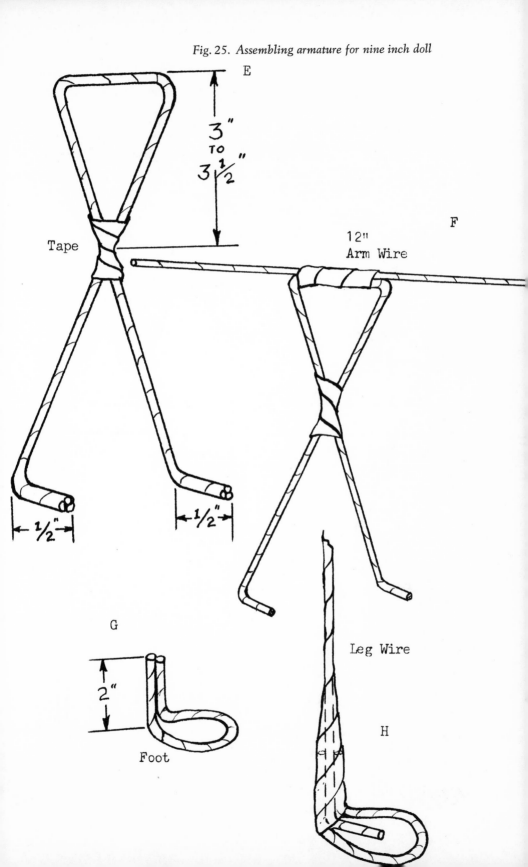

Fig. 25. *Assembling armature for nine inch doll*

E

3"
TO
3 1/2"

Tape

12"
Arm Wire

F

1/2"

1/2"

G

2"

Foot

Leg Wire

H

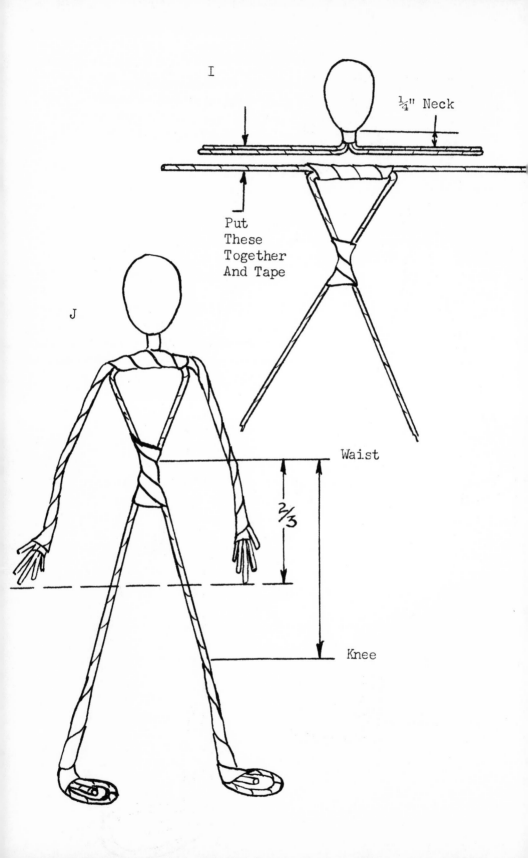

I

¼" Neck

Put
These
Together
And Tape

J

Waist

⅔

Knee

BODY PADDING AND WRAPPING

Padding for the bodies, arms and legs may be of raffia, cornhusks, nylon stockings, or other soft materials wrapped smoothly around the frame wires. Of course, the body is more heavily padded than the limbs, and, if it is a female figure, a bust and derriere may be added to give added interest to the figure.

STEP 1. ARMS: Start at the neck with several (six to eight) strands of raffia together and lay them on the arm wire down to the wrist. This gives some bulk or padding to wrap around. Holding this padding roughly in place, start wrapping the raffia back on itself, wrapping smoothly from the wrist back up across the shoulder to the neck. Hold ends with a clip clothes pin while you wrap the other arm in the same way. Now tie the raffia ends securely.

STEP 2. FEET: Pad feet before doing legs. Pad the top side of the feet by laying strands of raffia on the wire foot frame, leaving these strands long enough to reach up to the waist. Then wrap around both the wire and the padding strands, keeping the bottom or the sole flat so the figure will stand alone on its feet.

STEP 3. LEGS: This is done in the same manner as the arms. Starting at the waist, lay several strands of raffia down one leg wire. At the ankle, start wrapping the raffia smoothly back up to the waist, around both the raffia strands and the leg wire. Then do the other leg and fasten the raffia ends by tying together.

STEP 4. BODY: Holding ends of raffia at waist, lay the strands straight up across chest and wrap twice smoothly around neck. Bring strands down the back, under arm, and across the chest, then under the opposite arm. Continue wrapping upper torso down to the waist. Fasten the wrapping here using a fine (#32) wire or heavy thread wrapped very tightly several times around the waist. Snip off excess wrapping. Any extra padding or forming should be added now and wrapped again.

When all padding and wrapping is completed, bend the arms, fingers, elbows, knees, and body in a natural position. Bend wires with needle-nose pliers positioning each wire carefully.

WIGS

You will need rug yarn, string, flax, corn silk, or any other hair-like material your ingenuity may devise. (Fig. 26).

STEP 1. Determine the length of hair you wish. Measure a strand of string (or other material) over the top of the head and down on both sides to the length you want. Cut all the strands to this length and be sure to cut enough strands so they will cover the back of the head too.

STEP 2. Take a firm piece of tape (twill or similar kind) and measure from the hairline in front to a little beyond the crown. (In the case of braids, measure tape all the way down to the nape of the neck. This gives a part in the hair all the way down the back of the head.) Allow ½″ extra tape on each end (A).

STEP 3. Starting ½″ in from end of the tape, place the string or other material used across the tape. Keep tape centered across the strands and keep the strands close enough together so the tape doesn't show. Stitch in place by hand or (preferably) with a small stitch on the sewing machine (B).

Fig. 26. Making wig for doll

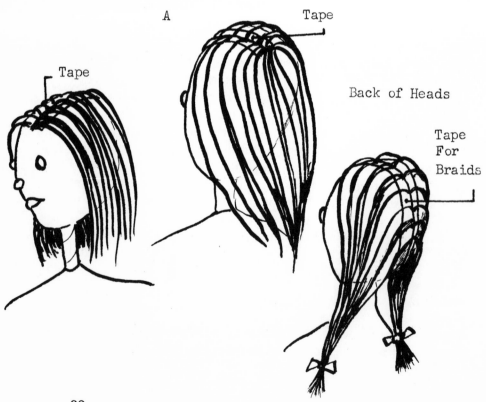

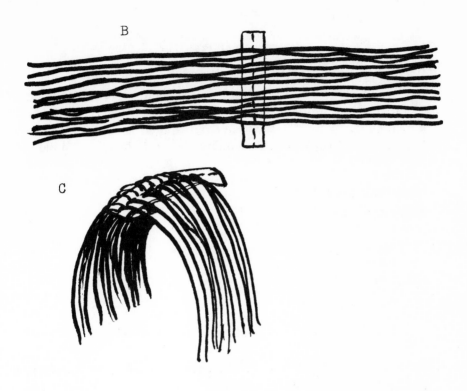

B

C

Step 4. Turn the front end of the tape under, so that it won't show at the hairline, and cement or stitch it in place (C). Cement the wig in place by putting cement along the underside of the tape, letting a little of this cement extend out into the hair to help hold it in place. Cement the back tab or end of tape flat to the back of the head, and then distribute strands of hair evenly around to cover the back. The wig is then trimmed and cut to suit the features.

SHOES

Dolls look much prettier if they are properly dressed, and shoes, being an important part of a costume, should be included. Doll shoes may be purchased at most toy shops or toy departments at the five-and-dime store. Choose a pair that will be a trifle larger than the doll's feet and the proper size for the particular doll. Partly fill the shoes with wet plaster of paris, push in the feet, and brace the figure in a standing position until the plaster is dry.

MEXICAN GROUP

Caballero, Senorita, "Bandolin", Burro. Plate 16 shows a charming bit of romance: Our Mexican caballero is serenading his senorita on his walnut "bandolin" (a cross between a banjo and a mandolin), while his Brazil-nut burro looks as balky as ever a burro looked. Instructions for making these delightful dolls follow.

MEXICAN CABALLERO

Materials Needed

> 1 wire armature for 9" doll (see beginning of this chapter)
> Raffia for padding and wrapping the armature
> 2 seeds or beads for eyes
> 1 seed or bead for nose
> Red paint for lips and mouth
> Black paint for hair
> Dried corn silk for mustache
> 1 pinecone for hat (from Southern short-leaf pine, red pine, pond pine)

STEP 1. MAKE BASIC DOLL: When you have the wire armature, pad and wrap it carefully with raffia. Because our caballero has no other clothing, make sure that the last raffia wrapping is particularly smooth, and continue wrapping his body down a little past the leg tops to make his tunic.

STEP 2. FEATURES: Cement the two seeds into the holes made for the eyes. With red paint, paint the inside of the hole for the mouth and allow a small margin around the mouth for the lips. Paint the hair on with black paint. Make his mustache from a little twist of corn silk and cement it on to decorate his upper lip.

STEP 3. HAT AND SARAPE: For his hat, cut or saw both ends off a pinecone, leaving a 2" piece from the middle. Remove all but one row of scales at the bottom of the piece. With a sharp knife, whittle the core of the cone to form a peak at the top. Sand smooth and then give it a coat of shellac. When dry, cement hat to top of head.

In the photo (Plate 16), he wears a sarape made of red-dyed melon seeds strung while wet, and woven together with a bead needle. A brightly colored piece of material would also be effective and, perhaps, simpler.

84

MEXICAN SENORITA

Materials Needed

1 wire armature for a 9-inch doll (see beginning of this chapter)
Raffia for padding and wrapping the armature
2 seeds or beads for eyes
1 seed or bead for nose
Red paint for lips
Flax, corn silk or any type yarn for hair
3 tiny strawflowers for hair decoration
1 pinecone scale (deodar, sugar or any cone with a large scale) for
    comb for hair
6 to 8 dried corn husks for skirt
Lamb's ear leaves for bodice
Colored raffia for sash and decorating skirt
1 skeletonized Japanese lantern (*Physalis*) for fan

STEP 1. MAKE BASIC DOLL: When you have completed the wire armature, pad and wrap it with raffia, place extra padding on the bust.

STEP 2. FEATURES: Cement the two seeds into the holes made for the eyes. For the nose, cement the seed into position, or, if a less protruding nose is desired, drill a hole and cement the seed partly down into the nose hole. Paint on her "rosebud" lips.

STEP 3. SKIRT, SASH AND BODICE: The senorita's skirt is made of cornhusks and is very bouffant. Cut off and discard both ends of 6 to 8 cornhusks. (The number of husks needed may vary considerably depending on their width and the size of the doll.) The remaining pieces should be long enough to reach from the doll's waist to her toes. Gather them at one end, across the grain, about ¼" in from the edge, overlapping each husk as it is added. With a

Plate 16. Mexican caballero with bandolin and burro, and his senorita

warm (not hot) iron, smooth out the husks. Move from the bottom toward the gathers. Do not press the gathers. Pull the gathering thread, adjust gathers around the doll's waist and fasten the thread securely.

Her sash is bright red raffia. To make the sash, wrap the body from under the bust down to and over the gathering thread of the skirt. Leave several long ends of raffia to reach the bottom of the skirt for sash ends.

Her bodice is made of two fresh lamb's ear leaves (*Stachys lanata*). Place the tip of one leaf at the right side of the figure at the waist. Lay the leaf up across the bust, over the left shoulder, down the back to the right side again. The second leaf is started at the left side of the waist, over the right shoulder and down the back to the left. The leaves overlap in back and are cemented together.

STEP 4. WIG: The senorita's hair is flax fibers, dyed brown. (For instructions, see *Wigs* in beginning of this chapter.) Her hair is long, extending partway down her back, and is pulled back and tied with a tiny raffia ribbon. She has a large golden comb in her hair at the top (a gilded scale from a deodar cone, with teeth cut into one end so it can be pushed into the hair). Place three small, bright red strawflowers in her hair and at the lower left side of her face.

A final touch is her "Spanish lace" fan. This is a skeletonized Japanese lantern (*Physalis*) that was pressed flat. A skeletonized magnolia leaf could be used as a substitute. The senorita is every inch an aristocrat! (Plate 16).

BANDOLIN

Materials Needed

> 1 medium-size walnut
> Piece of balsa wood, 4" x 1½" x ⅜" thick
> 4 pieces of wooden toothpicks, ½" long for pegs
> Small piece of wood, ½" x ¼" x ⅛" thick, for bridge
> White cotton thread
> Small piece of wooden toothpick for wedge
> 1 length of raffia, for neck cord

STEP 1. BODY OF INSTRUMENT: (Fig. 27). Split walnut in half along the natural line of division and remove nut meats. Place a generous amount of cement on the edge of one shell half and place it on the broad side of the balsa wood, rounded part flush with the end of the wood (*A*). Attach the other half in the same way on the other side of the wood (*B*). Hold in place with

Fig. 27. *Making bandolin and burro*

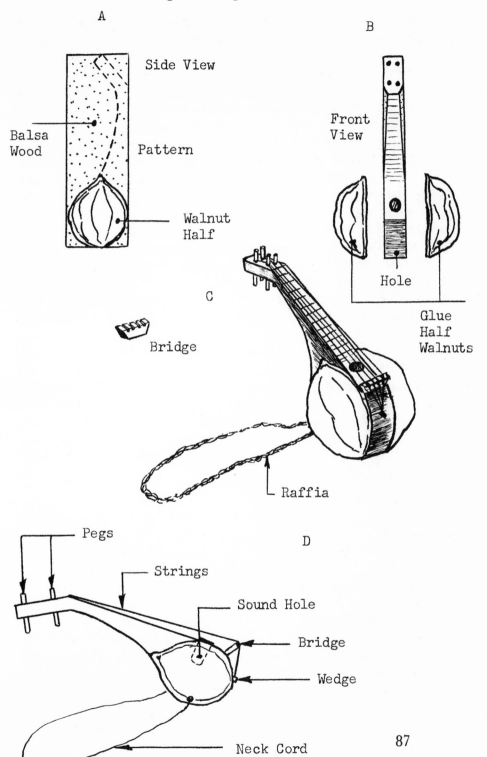

A

Side View

Balsa
Wood

Pattern

Walnut
Half

B

Front
View

Hole

Glue
Half
Walnuts

C

Bridge

Raffia

Pegs

Strings

Sound Hole

Bridge

Wedge

D

Neck Cord

87

rubber bands until thoroughly dry. With a sharp knife, whittle the wood into proper shape. See pattern in (A).

STEP 2. SOUND HOLE AND BRIDGE: Paint (with black) or drill a hole ¼" in diameter for the sound hole. See (B) and (D) for position of hole. For the bridge, cut a small piece of balsa wood ½" x ¼" x ⅛" thick, and cement the long edge of this to the carved balsa wood about ½" below the sound hole.

STEP 3. STRINGS: Drill four small holes for the toothpick pegs that will hold one end of the strings. To hold the other ends, drill another small' hole (which will hold the toothpick wedge) at the opposite end of the instrument, almost in the center of the bottom of the nut. Cement the toothpick pegs into their holes. Loop the cotton thread around the pegs and arrange it in position as strings. Cement the other ends of all four strings together and use the toothpick wedge to hold them in the small hole at the bottom of the nut (D).

STEP 4. NECK CORD: Drill a small hole through the lower part in back of the instrument, and run a piece of raffia through it for a neck cord.

BURRO

Materials Needed

> 2 Brazil nuts, one larger than other for body and head
> 2 pieces about 5" long #18 wire for legs
> 1 piece #26 wire, for attaching ears and neck, and making tail
> 2 scales 1½" long from any pinecone with scales long enough, for ears (sugar, long-leaf or Western white pine)
> Raffia
> Black paint

STEP 1. HEAD: Choose the size and shape of the nuts with their purpose in mind. Take the nut that will be the burro's head and drill a hole straight across the top of it for fastening the ears. For eyes, drill two larger holes about ½" forward of these ear holes, one on each side. Drill a hole straight across the neck end and pull a 4" to 5" piece of #26 wire through and twist it tightly. This will help to make the neck. See Fig. 27 (E).

STEP 2. BODY: Take the larger Brazil nut (the body) and drill a hole across the bottom of it at each end for legs. Drill a small hole straight into the end where the tail will be, and on the neck end, drill a hole across the nut for attaching the wires from the head (F).

STEP 3. ASSEMBLE: Wrap the two 5″ pieces of #18 wire with Floratape and push one wire through the front leg holes. Bend it down and shape for legs. Do the same with the other wire for back legs. Tape about 2″ of #26 wire and cement ½″ into the tail hole. Snip to proper length. Pull the neck wires, which are attached to the head, through the neck hole in the body, and fasten the head to the body tightly.

STEP 4. Wrap the legs, tail and neck with raffia (G). Make sure the neck is wrapped thick enough for the body.

STEP 5. FINISH: Wire the ears, one on each side of the head, with a piece of #26 wire. Shape the wire like a hairpin, slip it around one cone scale, push it through the hole drilled in the head, and twist it around the other cone scale to fasten (H). For eyes; seeds may be glued in the eye holes, or the holes may be painted black. Shellac the entire burro.

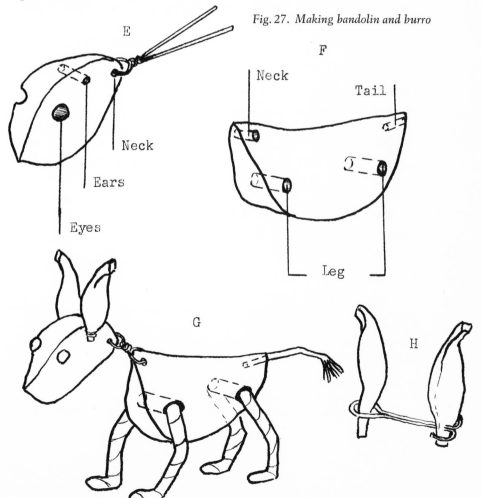

Fig. 27. *Making bandolin and burro*

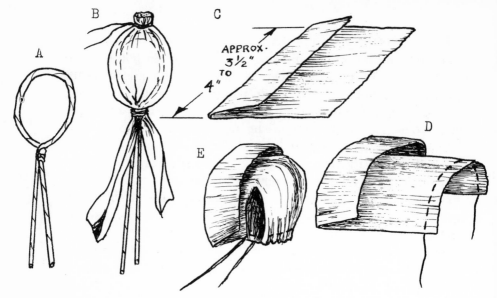

Fig. 28. Making cornhusk doll head and bonnet

CORNHUSK DOLLS

The cornhusk doll has become a part of our American heritage. In Grandma's day and before, many a little girl was delighted to receive a cornhusk doll. These dolls were made simply by taking a bundle of cornhusks of sufficient length to make body, legs and arms out of this one bunch. Each part was separated from the main body and tied into position with soft cotton yarn or thread. The materials were easily available and the dolls were charming and ready to take a lot of loving. Here are some present-day cornhusk dolls (with wire armatures for greater flexibility), that are certainly just as charming as the old-fashioned dolls. (Plate 17, Figure 28.)

Materials Needed

Wire armature
Cornhusks (worked damp)
Heavy cotton thread
Floratape
Black and red paint for features
Corn silk for hair
Acorn cap for his cap
Norway spruce cone scale, for his cap visor
Eucalyptus pod, for his pipe
Pipe cleaner for his pipe

90

If you are making both the cornhusk lady and the cornhusk gentleman, make two heads and two armatures as you go, remembering to give the gentleman broader shoulders, and to round the lady out a bit when you pad her.

STEP 1. MAKE HEAD: The head is made by forming a ball of cotton, old nylon stocking or cornhusks around a wire loop and then wrapping it with a wide cornhusk. Wrap an 8" piece of #18 wire with Floratape, and make a loop in it a little smaller than the size the head will be (A). Cover the wire loop with cotton or other padding to make a firm ball of a size to be in good scale with the body you are making. Now wrap the wide husk around the padding, gathering it together and tying it tightly with heavy thread at both the top and the bottom of the head. Snip the excess husks off the top (B).

STEP 2. MAKE BASIC DOLL: Make armature (see beginning of this chapter) using the cornhusk head you have just made. When you attach the head to the body, divide the cornhusks coming from the bottom of the head into two equal parts and spread them out to tape them, along with all the neck wires. Cornhusks instead of raffia may also be used for padding and wrapping the armature if desired. Paint or cement the features in place.

STEP 3. CLOTHES: Up to this point, the lady and the gentleman have been made in approximately the same way. Now let's make the difference.

CORNHUSK MAN

For trousers, make two tubes of cornhusks to reach from his waist to his ankles. Cement each tube together only from the crotch to the ankles, leaving the part from the crotch to the waist without cement. Slide the tubes onto his legs and cement the open parts of the tubes together where they overlap in the front and the back. His shirt is a wide husk pulled down over his shoulders front and back. (Cut a slit to get his head through.) Then cement or bind his shirt at the waist and cover with a belt (three thicknesses of husk folded and cemented in place). Make his cap from an acorn cap with the scale from a Norway spruce cone cemented on for a visor. His pipe is a euca pod on an inch stem piece of pipecleaner, both painted black.

CORNHUSK LADY

The lady's wig may be made from corn silk, darning cotton, shredded cornhusks, etc. (See section on *Wigs* in this chapter for instructions.) Put her sleeves on first, cementing husks into tubes and sliding them on the arms or just wrapping them around and fastening. Then make the bodice from two husks, each one passed across the front, over the shoulder and fastened at the waist back and front. For the skirt see *Mexican Senorita*, Step 3, Skirt. Make a sash from a piece of husk folded with the grain and cover the gathering threads of the skirt. Her cape is a wide piece of husk gathered at the neckline and tied in place. Her bonnet (Figure 28) is a piece of husk (measured across the grain) long enough to go around her face (C). The back edge is gathered with needle and thread (D). Then fold and shape it into a sunbonnet (E). Her basket was crocheted out of raffia.

LUFFA SPONGE DOLL

The luffa, or vegetable, sponge has many uses, from scrubbing cars to cleaning kitchens and baths; hence, one of its popular names is "vegetable dishrag". It also makes a great craft material.

Plate 17. Cornhusk dolls and an armature

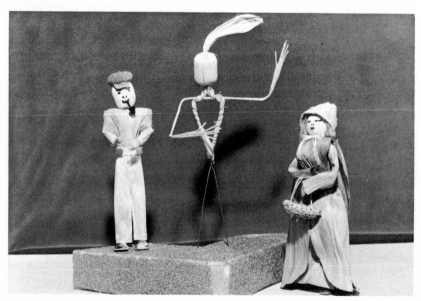

Plate 18. *Luffa sponge, luffa sponge lady, luffa sponge pitcher*

In warm climates, you can grow luffas in your garden. They are rather like a gourd with a hard, paper-like shell. When mature, they should be picked and dried, and the outer shell removed. Plate 18 (left) shows a luffa sponge after the outside papery shell has been removed. The doll is made from the same kind of sponge. (Plate 18, Fig. 29).

Materials Needed

> 2 luffa sponges outer shell removed
> Wrapping twine for neck and waist
> Embroidery cotton for features
> Brown yarn for hair
> Tape or ribbon for belt
> Papyrus or grass blossoms for hat trimming
> Doll shoes from the five-and-dime (optional)

The luffa sponge doll is the only doll in this group which does not need a wire armature since the sponge is strong enough to support itself. It will be much easier to shape and trim the sponge if you wet it and wring it out before starting to work.

STEP 1. MAKE BASIC FORM: One luffa sponge will make the head, body and legs or skirt of the doll. Cut the sponge so that it is about an inch longer than the height you want the doll. With strong thread, tie the end of the damp sponge tightly ½″ to 1″ down from the top (A). This makes a topknot (which will be trimmed off later) and, also, begins to shape the head. Be sure the thread is very tight so it won't slip off after the excess ends have been cut off.

About 1½″ further down (for a 9″ doll), start binding the wrapping twine tightly around the sponge for a neck. Continue binding for ½". The sponge must be squeezed in very tightly since the diameter must be small enough for the neck. This binding will be removed when the sponge is thoroughly dry.

Two inches below the neck, wrap twine around for the waist, pulling tightly enough to make the right size waist for your doll (A). When the sponge is dry, this twine, too, will be removed and replaced by a ribbon for a belt.

STEP 2. FEATURES AND WIG: With embroidery cotton, embroider the doll's eyes, eyebrows, nose and mouth. Trim the topknot on her head as close to the thread as possible without loosening the thread. Make her hair from brown yarn (see *Wigs*, beginning of this chapter). Secure the wig in position with two or three stitches through her head.

STEP 3. ARMS AND CLOTHES: Take the second luffa sponge, dampen it, and cut off the top small end (B). This small end, with its insides removed, will be her purse. Very carefully peel off the outer layer of sponge, which will be from ¼" to ½" thick. There is a natural separation inside the sponge, but even so, you will have to snip the membranes with scissors as you separate this outer layer from the inner core. It should come off evenly, all in one piece.

From the inner core you will get her arms. Snip off a 3½" to 4" length of this inner core. Split it lengthwise down the middle and roll each of these pieces into a tight roll big enough around to be her arm. Use strong thread to stitch the roll together, and then sew each arm to her body. Wrap a thread tightly around the wrist to form a hand.

On the outer layer of sponge which you have just peeled off, measure down 3½" from the cut-off top (B). Cut the sponge off evenly 3½" down all the way around. This piece will be her jacket. Turn it inside out (the inside has a kind of furry texture) and cut armholes. Use the luffa sponge material exactly as you would use any dress material, and make the doll's clothes. The jacket may need to be slit partway down the back with a "V" slit and sewed together again to shape it across her shoulders. Then trim the front lapels to a rounded line. You may want to fasten the jacket in place with a few stitches into the doll.

Cut and shape her hat from the outer sponge layer that remains (B). The decorations on the hat of the sponge doll in Plate 18 are papyrus blossoms lightly cemented into place.

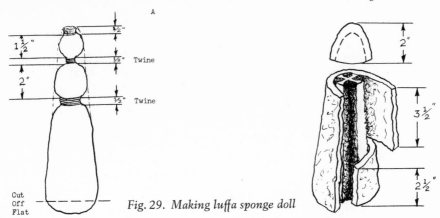

Fig. 29. Making luffa sponge doll

STEP 4. FINISHING TOUCHES: Complete her purse by pressing the hollowed-out end of the luffa sponge (while damp) under some heavy books. When dry, make a light braided raffia handle.

Dampen her arms and bend them at the elbow, using a pin-curl clip or some string to hold them in place until they are dry. Fasten her ribbon belt around her waist. If you want shoes to show under her skirt, fasten the doll's shoes carefully up into the sponge underneath.

EGGHEAD DOLLS

Mr. and Mrs. Egghead in their country best are an engaging pair! What you will need to make them is listed below. (Plate 19, Fig. 30).

Materials Needed

    1 wire armature for each doll (See directions in this chapter).
    Old nylon stockings for padding
    2 eggshells for heads
    Paraffin or old candle ends
    4 pieces, 18″ long, #22 wire for neck and shoulders
    Floratape
    Watermelon seeds (small) for his eyes
    Melon seeds for her eyes
    Day lily seed for his nose
    Poppy seeds for her nose, eyebrows, and his hair
    Pieces of castor-bean seedpod, for his eyebrows
    Acorn cap for his cap
    Deodar cone scale for his cap visor
    Spanish moss for her hair
    Strawflowers for her bouquet
    Hobby cement
    Red paint for mouths
    Doll shoes (from five-and-dime)
    Dress material scraps
    Blue denim scraps

If you are making both Mr. and Mrs. Egghead, it is easier to make two eggheads and two armatures as you work. When you make the armatures, remember that his shoulders are broader than hers, and when you pad the armatures give her a modest bust so that her clothes will hang nicely.

STEP 1. MAKE HEADS. PREPARE EGGS: To get an empty eggshell, "blow" the egg by making a small hole (¼" diameter) at both ends. Using the point of a sharp knife, be sure to pierce the surrounding sac, too. Holding egg over a bowl, blow out the white and the yolk. When the egg is empty, rinse the inside several times with cool water. Let the eggshells dry for several hours in a safe place. Snip four 7" pieces of #22 wire and wrap each wire separately with Floratape. About 1" down from one end, tape all four wires together for approximately 2½" (A).

Fig. 30. Wiring egghead for doll

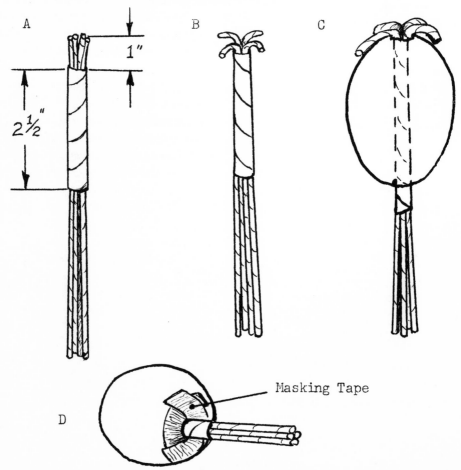

Masking Tape

Plate 19. Mr. and Mrs. Egghead

On the 1″ end, bend the four wires out and shape them into a little curved umbrella to fit the top of the egg (B). (This will be covered later by the hair.) Slide this wire unit down through the egg so that the curved wires lay smoothly on top of the egg (C). Holding the wires firmly in place, turn the egg upside down and with masking tape, cover the hole where the wire stem was inserted. Snug the tape close to the wires so that it won't leak when you pour hot paraffin into the egg (D). Melt some old candle ends or paraffin and run a tablespoon or two of the melted paraffin into the top hole of the egg. Shake the egg so that the paraffin covers the entire inner surface. Put in refrigerator to speed cooling. When set, add a few more spoonfuls of paraffin, shake again and as it cools, allow some of it to settle at the bottom of the egg. This will hold the wires in place when the paraffin has hardened. Cover the top curved wires with adhesive or masking tape.

Features: If you want the eyes to be shiny, shellac the seeds. Seeds for all features may be shellacked or not. Mr. Egghead's watermelon-seed eyes, day lily seed nose and castor bean seedpod eyebrows are all cemented in place. His poppy seed hair is cemented on by spreading cement where the hair will be and pressing the poppy seeds on. Paint his lips with red paint. Cement on his acorn cap with its deodar cone-scale visor.

Mrs. Egghead's melon seed eyes are first painted brown. Then cement on eyes, poppy seed nose and eyebrows (which are like his hair) and her Spanish moss hair. She too, has painted lips.

Remember that your eggheads are much more fragile than the other dolls and should be handled carefully.

STEP 2. MAKE BASIC DOLL: Make armature using the egghead you just made. (See *Armature For A 9" Doll,* in beginning of this chapter). Pad and wrap the armatures with old nylon hose until the bodies have the correct shape.

STEP 3. CLOTHES: All clothes are bits of materials leftover from dressmaking projects. Sew clothes as you would any doll's clothes, on the sewing machine or by hand. Cement doll shoes on their feet. Finally, add her bouquet of tiny strawflowers.

Fig. 31. Wiring apple head for doll

A

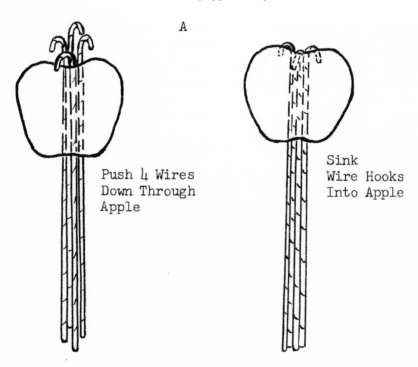

Push 4 Wires
Down Through
Apple

Sink
Wire Hooks
Into Apple

Plate 20.

APPLE HEADS

Due to the extensive drying time necessary for the apples, this is a project that is best worked in with other things. If the apple is left to dry naturally, it may take two months (depending on climate). However, the carved head may also be dried by leaving it in a very slow oven (150° or less) for three or four days. Making apple heads can be a family project, each person trying his hand at being a sculptor. A paring knife will be your tool and an apple your medium. (Plate 20, Fig. 31).

Materials Needed

    1 apple
    2 pieces, each 18″ long, #18 wire
    2 seeds or beads for eyes
    Yarn, for eyebrows and wig
    Powdered rouge for cheeks and lips

STEP 1. MAKE HEAD: Select a firm, ripe apple with no bruised or rotten spots. Peel it smoothly and evenly, and dip it in lemon juice to help keep its light color. Carve the features into the apple using the tip of a sharp knife. It is good to exaggerate the features slightly, the eye sockets deeper, nose larger, etc., to compensate for the distortion as the apple shrinks in drying. When the carving is finished, dip it in lemon juice once more. Now put in the wires which will later be the means of attaching the apple head to the doll body. These wires are put in before the apple dries, because as the apple shrinks it will hold the wires more tightly than if they were put in after it had dried.

Individually tape four 8" pieces of #18 wire, make a small "U" hook on one end of each, and push each wire through the apple until the hook is firmly down into the apple. These wires will have to be put in close around the core since the core itself is too hard to push a wire through (A).

Set the apple head aside to dry, and occasionally check it and pinch the features back into place. Since the apple shrinks as it dries, the features will change, but they will retain their character.

After the head is dry, wrap several layers of tape around the neck wires to keep the head from slipping down on the wires. Cement seeds or beads into the eye sockets and use yarn for eyebrows. A little powdered rouge will put color into the cheeks and lips. Finally, a wig of yarn or other material (see *Wigs,* in this chapter), will complete your apple head. When you have done this, make it into a doll. (See *Armature For A 9" Doll* and *Body Padding and Wrapping,* in this chapter.) Make clothes for your doll to suit the character you have created.

4. CRAFTY CRITTERS

The woods and fields are alive with interesting creatures, all kinds and sizes of birds, frogs, rabbits, turtles, and a host of others. In the same woods and fields, you find a wide range of plant materials from which to craft these delightful little creatures. Pine, hemlock, spruce and fir trees—all yield cones of varying sizes and shapes which can be used for your craft projects.

Scotch pine will furnish many cones of medium to small size. These cones are easy to obtain in good color since the tree obligingly drops the cones before they become weathered. Scotch pine cones are very sturdy and are a good size for many natural craft projects. The tree ranges from western North Carolina to Quebec and across the Lake States to Saskatchewan and northwestern Nebraska.

Hemlock cones are not woody, but quite soft and small. To obtain the best-colored cones, you will have to pick them off the tree as soon as, or just before, they have opened up. The hemlock tree has a range from Maine to northeastern Minnesota and southward along the mountains from Pennsylvania and West Virginia to northern Georgia and Alabama.

White spruce are soft cones, about two inches long by one-half inch in diameter. The scales are quite close together. As with the hemlock, these cones must be picked off the tree for optimum color. The white spruce ranges from Alaska across the Lake States, through New York and New England.

Australian pine produces small, woody, deeply striated cones, rather longer than wide and somewhat flat on both ends. Many and varied are the projects in which they can be used. This tree grows in Florida and California, but the cones of the California trees are much larger than the Florida ones. These cones may be purchased, if you don't live where they grow.

Red pine, white pine; blue spruce and Norway spruce. All of these are rather common especially in the Northeastern states, so a cone supply should be easy to find. Of course the bright un-weathered color is preferred, but cones will readily take a coat of paint, shellac or varnish, so if the fresh ones are not available, the weathered ones will do. In any case, do not use cones that have lost their strength and firmness. Be careful to pick only the best and, when the opportunity presents itself, gather as many cones as are available. If possible, pick some that are closed, too.

Teasels grow wild in most parts of the country, but you may grow them in your garden. They are biennials and may grow to six feet tall.

Burdock has small, round, prickly balls and it, too, is very common along roadsides and near old deserted buildings.

Acorns in a very wide range of size, shape and texture are found everywhere. Not all kinds will be in one location, but enough for most uses can be found almost anyplace.

Sea-oats grow along the seashore from Canada to Texas. They can be purchased if none grow near you.

Eucalyptus trees grow mainly in Florida and California. There are many varieties, and the pods vary greatly in size and shape. These, too, can be purchased if none grow near you.

Butternuts still flourish in some sections of the country. They are really very worthwhile from the standpoint of both color and texture.

Melon, squash and pumpkin seeds are available anywhere. If you don't have the actual fruit or vegetable, you may purchase a packet of seeds intended for planting.

Hemerocallis or day lily can furnish you with a wide selection of seedpods, some small, some closed, some large and some open. Letting the seed form does no harm to the plant. Be sure to save the seeds as they are very black and shiny and make excellent eyes for your creatures.

Martynia (sometimes called unicorn plant or devil's claw) may be grown in the garden. It is an easy-to-grow annual with a rather pretty flower and a most interesting seedpod. The pods can also be purchased.

Hare's tail grass grows wild in some sections of the country, but in New York State we grow it in the garden. It is a delightful, easy-to-grow annual and is very useful.

Jacaranda pods and Cocos plumosus fruit are grown in Florida and California. They can be purchased.

TEASEL CREATURES
(Bear, Bunny, Lion, Teasel-Martynia Goat)

Teasels should be picked before they have lost their nice fresh color. This is just about the time when the little lavender blooms are gone. Store the teasels for a week or two in a sheltered place to dry. When dry, clean them with a brush to remove any dead flowers or other debris. Tap them firmly against your hand to dislodge the seeds. Cleanliness is essential for a quality product. Cut the curling bracts and stem off each of the teasels except the one to be used for the lion's head. (Plates 21-24).

The eyes, ears, and nose of any of these teasel creatures may be made of Play-Doh or modeling clay, if the recommended seeds, movable eyes, or other accessories are difficult to obtain. Eyes and nose are small round bits that are pressed into the spines and cemented. Ears are molded in the right size and shape for the particular creature being made. You may find movable eyes and other accessories at a hobby shop.

TEASEL BEAR

Materials Needed

> 1 large teasel for body
> 2 medium-size teasels, 1 for head, 1 for hind legs
> 2 smaller teasels for front legs
> 2 hemerocallis seeds for eyes
> 1 albizzia seed for nose
> 2 pistachio nut shells (halves) for ears (matched for size and shape)
> Cement

STEP 1. BODY: The largest teasel is used for the body. The cut end (the stem end) is the bottom of the bear's body.

STEP 2. HIND LEGS: Cut one medium-size teasel in half from stem end to tip. Put the cut side down and cement one half on each side of the stem end of the largest teasel, keeping the pointed end to the front. Place the halves so the large teasel will stand upright without additional support.

STEP 3. FRONT LEGS: Cement the two smaller teasels, one on each side, near the top of the body and directly over the ones on the bottom. Again, keep the pointed end forward.

STEP 4. HEAD: If the remaining medium teasel is more than 1½″ long, cut it down to this length. Cement this to the top of

Plate 21. A pair of teasel bears

the body with the cut end to the front. Let the cement dry thoroughly.

STEP 5. FEATURES: For eyes, snip a few of the spines off each side of the face and cement the two hemerocallis seeds there. Cement the albizzia seed over the center of the cut surface in front for the nose. For ears, cement the pistachio nut halves in position.

TEASEL BUNNY

Materials Needed

> 1 medium-size teasel for body
> 3 small teasels for head and legs
> 1 tiny teasel for tail
> 2 large squash seeds or 2 pistachio nut shells for ears
> 2 hemerocallis seeds for eyes
> 1 red sandalwood seed for nose
> Cement

STEP 1. BODY: Choose the appropriate size teasel for a body.

STEP 2. LEGS: Cut two of the small teasels in half from stem end to tip. Cement these halves a little to each side of the larger teasel, two near the front or tip end and the other two toward the back end. The medium-size or body teasel should be in a horizontal position.

STEP 3. TAIL: Cement the tiny teasel to the stem end of the body for a tail.

STEP 4. HEAD: Cement the remaining small teasel to the pointed end of the body for the head, stem end forward.

Step 5. features: Cement ears, eyes and nose in position as for the teasel bear.

TEASEL LION

Northern teasels, as opposed to western teasels, are used to make this lion. The northern teasel has long curling bracts which are necessary for the lion's mane, while the western teasel has few, if any, bracts.

Materials Needed

> 1 large teasel for body
> 2 medium-size teasels for legs
> 1 medium-size teasel with curling bracts for head
> Curling bracts from 3 teasels for ruff
> Moving eyes
> 1 piece wire for tail
> Tuft of grass for tail
> Brown Floratape
> Cement

Step 1. body: Select the appropriate size teasel for the body.

Step 2. legs: Cut each of the two medium-size teasels in half from stem end to tip. The front legs may be shortened, or, use a slightly smaller teasel for them. Cement the stem end of each half onto the body, with the cut side away from the body, so that the lion will stand on all fours.

Plate 22. A pair of teasel bunnies

Plate 23. Teasel lion

STEP 3. TAIL: Using brown tape, tape a tuft of grass onto one end of a short piece of wire. Continue taping the rest of the wire so no wire is exposed. Cement the tail in the proper position.

STEP 4. HEAD AND FEATURES: Take the medium-size teasel with the curling bracts still attached. Using a razor blade, cut a slit straight across the tip end in a horizontal position for the mouth. Cement the moving eyes into position.

STEP 5. RUFF: Carefully cut the curling bracts (in one piece) from the base of three teasels. Cement these three bracts onto the back of the curling bract on the lion's head. Arrange the bracts to make his ruff as full as possible.

STEP 6. ASSEMBLE: Cement head onto body.

TEASEL-MARTYNIA GOAT

Materials Needed

    1 medium to large teasel for body
    2 or 3 martynia pods for head and legs
    2 martynia seeds for eyes
    2 sections of a beechnut burr for ears
    1 pistachio nut shell for nose
    1 cattail stem (⅜" diameter) 1½" long for wedge for head
    1 clematis seed cluster for tail
    Cement
    White paint
    Black paint
    1 piece of pipe cleaner 3 inches long for neck

STEP 1. HEAD: Shorten the claws of the martynia pod selected for the goat's head to approximately 1½″. Make a wedge out of the cattail stem by slicing diagonally down the length of it. Carefully spread the claws of the "head" pod apart and cement in the cattail stem wedge with the broad part of the wedge at the top of the head. Bend the pipe cleaner in half and, starting with the bend at the top, cement about ½″ down against the cattail wedge in the back of the head. This will leave a small bit of pipe cleaner neck extending below the head to be cemented into the teasel body later.

STEP 2. FEATURES: Cement on the martynia seeds for eyes, the beechnut burrs for ears, and the pistachio nut shell for the nose.

STEP 3. LEGS, BODY AND TAIL: From the other two martynia pods, select claws that will make four 2″ legs. The two hind legs should have a heavy thigh section made from claws clipped close to the pod. Cement the legs to the teasel body, the hind legs closer to each other than are the front legs. Cement the clematis seed cluster on for the tail.

STEP 4. ASSEMBLE AND PAINT: When the cement on the body and head parts is thoroughly dry, cement the pipe cleaner neck into position on the teasel body above and between the forelegs. Paint the legs and horns black and brush black paint over the teasel and lightly down the face. Paint the eyes black with a white rim.

PINECONE CREATURES
(Horned Owl, Abstract Creature, Woodland Pixies, Quail, Mice, Tropical Fish, Reluctant Dragon, Owl on Nut and Mint Cup, Big Barn Owl)

TO CLEAN CONES: All cones should be thoroughly cleaned before you use them. A medium-stiff paint brush makes a good tool for cleaning dust and dirt out of the scales. The cones may be washed in water if necessary, but wash only a few at a time as they close up when they are wet. However, they will reopen as they dry. If the cones are covered with pitch, they may be cleaned in turpentine or mineral spirits. Either of these will give a clean, fresh look to all cones. (Plates 25-33).

TO REMOVE SCALES FROM CONES: Most scales may be removed from the cones by breaking off the tip of the cone first. Then, by using a twisting, pulling motion, the scales may be pulled off one by one. Use heavy shears to snip the scales off if they cannot be removed by pulling.

BIG BARN OWL

This barn owl stands about eight inches tall, almost life-size. A single longleaf pinecone should be selected for its owl-like qualities — in this case, the position of the round mass of unopened scales at the stem end of the cone. This round mass will be the head. Since the owl will be much more convincing if the face is to the front, pick a cone in which this mass slants decidedly forward.

Materials Needed

> 2 longleaf pinecones
> 2 artificial eyes with moving pupils
> 1 radish seedpod for beak

STEP 1. BODY: After selecting the body cone, cut out the tip end and spread out and flatten the scales at the bottom so the owl will stand firmly with his face slanting as much to the front as possible.

STEP 2. WINGS AND TUFTS: Using the second cone as a source of extra scales, extend wings out on either side and cement them in place. Add a few shorter scales for the tufts on the owl's head.

STEP 3. FEATURES: Cement the artificial eyes and the radish pod beak in place.

Plate 25. Big barn owl and horned owl

HORNED OWL

Materials Needed

    1 short-leaf pinecone for body
    1 spruce cone for head
    2 cotton pod sections for horns
    2 kernels of yellow corn for eyes
    2 milkweed pods (open) for wings
    1 milkweed pod section for beak
    Cement

STEP 1. BODY: Cut or break scales from the tip end of the shortleaf pinecone so that it will stand solidly.

STEP 2. HEAD: Cut or break scales from the tip end of the spruce cone so that it will fit solidly when attached to the stem end of the body cone. Cement head to body.

STEP 3. FEATURES: For horns, cement cotton pod sections, one on each side of the top of the head. Cement corn kernel eyes in appropriate position. For the beak, cement a section of milkweed pod in place. Cement milkweed pod wings, one on each side of body, at stem end of the shortleaf pinecone.

ABSTRACT CREATURE

Materials Needed

    1 white spruce cone (closed) for head
    1 white spruce cone (open) for body
    2 pointed eucalyptus pods for legs
    1 hemlock cone for tail
    2 grains of wheat for eyes
    Cement

Plate 26. Abstract creature

STEP 1. CEMENT HEAD TO BODY: The *closed-cone* head should be used with its scales facing forward. The scales of the *open-cone* body should face backward. Cement these two cones together in the position shown in Plate 26.

STEP 2. LEGS: For legs, tuck the stem ends of the eucalyptus pods up under the creature's chest scales, one on each side, and cement them there.

STEP 3. TAIL AND EYES: Cement the hemlock cone to tip end of the body cone for the tail. Cement wheat grains in proper position for eyes.

WOODLAND PIXIES

Little woodland pixies are delightfully appealing creatures. Each one is mounted on half of a butternut shell.

Materials Needed

> 2 Scotch pine cones for bodies
> 2 acorns for heads
> 2 butternut halves for bases or stands
> 1 hemerocallis pod for girl's hat
> 1 acorn cap for boy's cap
> 1 sugar pine cone scale for peak of boy's cap
> 1 pipe cleaner to attach heads to bodies
> Red paint for lips
> Black paint for eyes and eyebrows
> Cement

STEP 1. HEAD AND BODY: The tip of the acorn will be a pixie's nose and the flat end which was covered by the acorn cap will be the back of his head. Holding the acorn so that the nose will be facing front, drill or pierce a hole for the pipe cleaner neck underneath and to the back of each acorn. Drill a hole in the stem end of each Scotch pinecone. The holes should be about a half inch deep. Cut two one-inch pieces of pipe cleaner. Cement one-half-inch of each piece of pipe cleaner into each of the acorns and attach the heads to the bodies by cementing the other half-inch into the holes in the cones.

STEP 2. BASE: Cement the tip end of the Scotch pinecones onto the curved side of the butternut halves so that they will stand solidly upright. Brace them in position until the cement dries.

STEP 3. FEATURES: Paint the eyes and eyebrows on each pixie head using black paint, and with red paint make the lips. The

Plate 27. Woodland pixies

acorn tip nose may be accentuated with a touch of paint, either red or black.

STEP 4. HATS: The girl pixie wears a most becoming hat, which is an empty hemerocallis seedpod. Clean all seeds and fine membranes out of the pod; (save the seeds for creature's eyes). Trim and shape the open end and then fit and cement the pod to the acorn at the most becoming angle.

The boy pixie wears a cap made of an acorn cap with the scale of a sugar pine cone trimmed to shape and cemented in place for the peak.

QUAIL

Materials Needed

> 1 Scotch pine cone (open) for body
> 4 pieces, 9" long, #26 wire for legs and feet
> Brown Floratape
> Clay, Play-Doh, papier maché or any commercial material used for model making; for head
> 2 cotton pod sections for wings
> 2 small black seeds for eyes
> White paint
> Brown paint
> Cement

STEP 1. LEGS AND FEET: Once you master the art of feet and balance, the rest of the bird is quite simple. The quail's legs will be short; only long enough to hold the body off the table. The legs and feet are all made from one group of wires: Tape the full length of each of the four wires. Holding all four taped wires together, start taping one inch from one end and tape the four together down to one inch from the other end. About halfway up the body cone, wrap the middle of the taped wires around the cone and pull it down into the scales. Use a little cement to hold the wires to the scales of the cone. This will leave two wires of equal length coming down out of the cone for legs. If legs are too long, allow enough wire for bending back the toes and cut off the rest. Remove enough of the tape holding the four wires together to have one inch free to bend out for the toes.

To make the toes, bend one inch of one wire back at a right angle and bend the three remaining wires forward. Spread the toes on both feet so the bird will stand by itself.

STEP 2. HEAD AND FEATURES: The head may be made of clay,

Play-Doh, papier maché or any commercial material used for making models. Mold the head on the "body" cone so that it fits snugly. Press the seeds that are being used for eyes into position in the clay. Paint the head a suitable shade of brown to harmonize with the cones unless the clay is already a pleasing color. Use white paint to make the markings. (*Note:* a small cone such as one from Australian pine, may also be used for the head, with seeds for eyes and stem for beak.)

STEP 3. WINGS: Cotton pod sections make attractive wings. Trim the stem end of two cotton pod sections flat and push this flattened end under the scales near the front of the body cone. Cement them in place, one on each side, pointing backwards.

Plate 28. Quails

MICE

These adorable little mice are approximately life-size and are quite real looking.

Materials Needed

1 Scotch or Red pinecone (unopened) for body and head
Darning cotton for whiskers
2 small scales Norway spruce for ears
2 small round seeds for eyes
2 small scales Scotch pinecone for feet
1 piece grape tendril for tail
Black enamel paint for eyes
Cement

Plate 29. Scotch pinecone

STEP 1. WHISKERS: The unopened Scotch or Red pinecone serves as both body and head of the mouse. Drill a small hole straight through the tip of the nose. Pull the darning cotton through this hole and clip it to about one-half inch on each side. Cement it in place and spread the strands on both sides to make the whiskers. A little glue or shellac will stiffen the thread so he will not have limp whiskers.

STEP 2. EARS AND EYES: About half an inch back from the whiskers, saw small slits in the cone to hold the ears. Cement Norway spruce scales upright in the slits with the concave side toward the nose.

For eyes, cement small round seeds in place. Using a very small brush, paint the eyes with black enamel. Two coats of paint may be needed to achieve the beady effect necessary for realism.

STEP 3. FEET AND TAIL: Position Scotch pine scales for front feet to balance the mouse (the feet can be any little wedge of material which will hold the tip of the cone up off the table). Cement the feet in place. For the tail, drill or pierce a small hole at rear of mouse. Cement a small piece of grape tendril in the hole (a small piece of other vine, or even a taped piece of wire) may be used for the tail.

PINECONE TROPICAL FISH

A tropical fish can be made by a young child, and is most attractive. (Plate 30.)

Materials Needed

1 Scotch pinecone, (unopened) for head and body
2 crabeye seeds for eyes
4 Shortleaf pinecone scales for fins and tail
Cement

STEP 1. BODY AND EYES: To anchor the crabeye seeds firmly, gouge out a small depression in the large end of the cone where the eyes will be. Cement the seeds, (with the black dot showing for pupils), into position.

STEP 2. FINS AND TAIL: Cut slits in the "body" cone to hold the fins and tail. Trim the scales of Shortleaf pine cone to the desired shape and cement them into the slits.

Fasten a bit of thread onto the back of both of these fish and suspend them so they can "swim" around in the air for everyone's amusement.

Plate 31. Reluctant dragon

RELUCTANT DRAGON

Materials Needed

> 1 Norway spruce cone for body
> 1 large jacaranda pod (open) for head
> 1 medium jacaranda pod (open) for hind legs
> 1 small jacaranda pod (open) for front legs
> 2 swamp buttons for eyes
> 2 tallow berry sections for teeth
> 1 mahogany pod section for tail
> Black paint for eye pupils
> Cement

STEP 1. HEAD AND BODY: Cement swamp button eyes on top of the jacaranda pod near the stem end. Inside the dragon's mouth (the open end of the jacaranda pod), cement his tallow berry teeth. Cement the head onto the stem end of the Norway spruce cone "body." Paint pupils on the eyes with black paint.

STEP 2. LEGS AND TAIL: Split the small and medium jacaranda pods in half. Cement the small jacaranda pod halves about an inch below the head for front legs, keeping the inside of the pods toward the body. For back feet, cement the two medium pod halves a little under the bottom front of the cone. Cement the stem end of the mahogany pod section under the cone for the tail. Adjust back feet and tail to provide good balance.

OWL ON NUT AND MINT CUP

This little owl may be made into a lapel pin, glued to the top of a pencil, or used to decorate any number of things. In the photograph (Plate 32), he adorns a nut and mint cup.

Materials Needed

> 1 large Australian pinecone for body
> 1 small Australian pinecone for head
> 3 apple or pear seeds for ears and beak
> 2 tiny round shells for eyes
> 2 coquina shell halves for wings
> Cement
> Black paint for eye pupils
> White paint for nut and mint cup
> 2 open milkweed pods, large and medium, for cups
> 3 pieces, 9" long, #22 wire for nut and mint cup
> White Floratape

114

STEP 1. OWL: Cement the small Australian pinecone onto the larger one to make a head on a body. Two apple or pear seeds cemented into position make ears, while another apple or pear seed becomes his beak. Cement tiny round shells into place for eyes and paint the pupils on with black paint. Cement coquina shell halves onto either side of the body cone for the wings.

STEP 2. NUT AND MINT CUP: Give each milkweed pod a wire stem and cover it with white Floratape. (See Strange Flowers, How to Wire and Tape, Chapter V.) Curve the taped wire stem of the larger pod down and around to make it sit level on the table. Hold the smaller pod in position above the first one and bend its wire stem down to join and follow the first stem. Tape the two wires together. A wire handle may be added to achieve better stability. For this, cover a third wire with white Floratape, bend it to the desired shape and tape it in position.

STEP 3. ASSEMBLE: To attach the owl to the nut and mint cup, it may be necessary to use a small ball of clay. The rim of the milkweed pod is too narrow to afford a good surface for cementing.

Plate 32. Owl on nut and mint cup

BLACK WALNUT FROG

This miniature creature will delight all who like tiny things. The materials are simple and he can be made rather quickly (Plate 33).

Materials Needed

> 1 black walnut or butternut for head and body
> 1 green chenille stem or pipe cleaner for legs
> 2 small eucalyptus pods for eyes
> Green paint
> Yellow paint
> Sandpaper
> Cement

STEP 1. HEAD AND BODY: Shape the black walnut or butternut to more closely resemble a frog by sanding the tip end smooth and flat for his chest. With green and yellow paint, make a green frog with a yellow under-belly. Paint the outside of the two small eucalyptus pods yellow and cement them in place for eyes when the paint is dry.

STEP 2. LEGS: Cut chenille stem or dyed pipe cleaner into two 1″ pieces and two 2″ pieces. Shape these pieces into legs, the 1″ ones for the front and the 2″ ones for the back. Cement into place and when dry, adjust the legs so the frog will sit on the table.

Plate 34. Summer squash duck

SUMMER SQUASH CREATURES

(Duck and Whale)

Summer squash belong to the gourd family, but when buying seeds you must ask for it by name. Crookneck Summer Squash not only make interesting containers, but also some very clever little creatures (Plates 34 and 35).

If you are fortunate enough to have a garden, do plant some of this squash, and do not eat them all; allow some to mature on the vine. In autumn when the weather has turned cold (about the end of October), cut the squash off the vine, leaving a short stem on the squash. Put them in a cold, dry place (a garage will do). Do not pile them on top of one another as they must have good air circulation. Leave them undisturbed until spring; it will take that long to dry them.

Never use the squash before it has dried. Before cutting a dried summer squash for the various creatures or containers, scrub it with hot soapy water and a stiff brush. Rinse the squash and let it stand in a damp towel for several hours. This softens it and takes away some of the brittleness that may cause it to split when you are sawing or cutting it with a knife. It can also be cut with shears by snipping it a little snip at a time. While it is in the damp towel, keep checking it from time to time and do not allow it to get waterlogged. After cutting, be sure to dry the squash thoroughly again before cementing or painting it.

If, when cut, the shell slips off and leaves the inner spongy part of the squash intact, it, too, can be used. A coat of white shellac will add materially to its strength.

Since the smooth surface of the summer squash may present difficulties in getting some materials to adhere well to it, small bits of cotton saturated in cement will aid in establishing a bond.

SUMMER SQUASH DUCK

Select the squash for the duck carefully. In the photograph (Plate 34), the whole squash with the stem had a perfect form for a duck. The shape of the squash that will be used for wings and feet is unimportant.

Materials Needed

> 1 dried crookneck summer squash with short stem for head and body
> 1 dried crookneck summer squash for wings, feet and tail
> 2 black thumbtacks or black-painted pumpkin seeds for eyes
> White paint
> Cotton
> Cement

STEP 1. DUCK'S BILL: For the bill, use a razor blade or small saw to split the stem up to the squash. Pry it open carefully to resemble an open bill. Force a seed or pebble between the two parts of the bill to hold it open. When dry, the seed can remain in position.

STEP 2. CUT TAIL, FEET AND WINGS: Saw a shallow, rounded piece off the large end of the second squash for a tail. Cut two duck-foot-shaped pieces from the same squash, using heavy shears and making only a small snip at a time so it does not crack or break in the wrong place. Cut two wings, a right and a left. They should be similar, but not necessarily exactly alike. Let the cut pieces dry thoroughly.

STEP 3. ASSEMBLE: Place the shallow, round tail piece flat side down on the table and, using small bits of cotton, cement it under and behind the body. Cement the feet in position in front. Between these three pieces the duck should stand balanced. Cement wings in the desired position, also using cotton.

STEP 4. PAINT AND EYES: When dry, paint the duck white and cement his black eyes in place.

SUMMER SQUASH WHALE

Select a squash that has a small protrusion on the tip end for a snout and a curved stem end for a tail.

Plate 35.

Materials Needed

> 1 crookneck dried summer squash for head and body
> 1 small areca palm boot or piece of melaleuca bark or cornhusk—for tail and fins
> 2 Pinyon pine seeds for eyes
> Black paint for eyes
> Cotton
> Cement

STEP 1. BODY: Place squash on a table with the tail end curving upward. With coarse sandpaper, sand the underpart of the squash if it is necessary to make the whale stay balanced.

STEP 2. TAIL AND FINS: Cut a slit in the stem end of the squash. With shears, shape the tail from the wide end of a small areca boot or other material. Cement it into the slit. For fins, cut two wedge-shaped pieces from the remainder of the areca boot or other material. Position the fins on each side of the body, about one-third of the distance from the snout, with the wide side of the fin away from the body and pointing toward the tail. Using cotton, cement them in place.

STEP 3. EYES: For eyes, cement two pinyon pine seeds in the desired position. Paint in pupils with black paint.

MARTYNIA POD CREATURES
(Fighting Birds, Crane, Dragon, Owl, Flamingo and Deer)

The curious martynia pod, also known as devil's claw, offers exciting creative possibilities. The long, graceful, curved claws give a bold dramatic line to any creature made from them (Plates 36-38).

MARTYNIA FIGHTING BIRDS

Materials Needed for Two

> 5 martynia pods with stems at least ½" long
> 4 button eucalyptus pods for eyes
> Black paint
> Yellow paint
> Cotton
> Cement

STEP 1. ASSEMBLE HEAD TO BODY: Fit the stem of one martynia pod into the seed opening between the claws of another pod. *Note:* It may be necessary to remove a few seeds from the second pod so the first pod will fit into it. Place the bottom or body pod so that the claws turn back and up. The claws on the head pod should curve down and out to the front as belligerent wings. Try different pods until the position and fit are satisfactory.

To cement these two pods together, place a generous amount of cement on the stem of the bottom pod. Wrap a small piece of cotton around the cemented stem, cover the cotton with more cement, and push the stem into position in the other pod. Make both birds this way and set them aside for the cement to dry.

STEP 2. LEGS: Cut the claws off the last pod and cut them to the correct length for legs, approximately two inches long. Cement these, one on each side, to the front of the body so that the bird will stand alone.

STEP 3. BEAK AND EYES: Split the stem on the head pod with a razor blade and separate the halves carefully for a beak. Cement the eucalyptus pod eyes in place.

STEP 4. PAINT: The fighting birds may be painted to simulate the brightly-colored birds of the tropics or, to give a more somber effect, painted black like the "blackbirds" in the photograph, (Plate 36). Paint the beaks yellow.

MARTYNIA CRANE

Many and varied birds can be crafted from the martynia pod. Here is a crane.

Materials Needed

> 2 martynia pods for body and wings
> 1 small peanut for head
> 4 pieces, 18″ long, #26 wire for legs, toes and neck
> 2 hemerocallis seeds for eyes
> 1 piece, 2″ long, of dried gladiolus or cattail leaf for beak
> White paint
> Black paint
> Cement
> Cotton

STEP 1. BODY: Cut all the stem off the pod that will be the bird's body. Then drill a hole for the neck wires straight into the end of the pod where the stem was. Drill another hole from side

Plate 36. Martynia pod fighting birds

to side about 1″ to 1½″ down from the stem end. The leg wires will be pushed through here.

STEP 2. LEGS AND TOES: Cover each of the four 18″ wires individually with Floratape and then cut each one into one 12″ piece and one 6″ piece. Tape the four 12″ pieces of wire together, leaving 2″ to 3″ untaped on each end. These unjoined ends will be spread out later to make toes. Insert this 12″ taped wire piece into the hole for the legs, center it and bend both ends down close to the body. Make sure the bird's tail feathers are pointing up. Determine the length of the legs (both neck and legs are about equal length and are approximately the same length as the body), then allow an additional inch or more for the toes, and cut off the leg wires at that point. Bend two toes forward and two back and spread them all apart. Bird's knees go back (not forward) so bend the legs to the back about halfway down.

STEP 3. HEAD AND NECK: Tape the four remaining 6″ lengths of wire together to make the neck. If it isn't thick enough, pad it with more tape or tape a pipe cleaner in with the wires.

Pierce a hole in the underside of the small peanut. The hole should be large enough to allow the end of the neck wire to enter. Cut a slit across the opposite end of the peanut from side to side to hold the beak. Drill holes in position for the seed eyes. Place cement on one end of the taped neck wires and insert it in the neck hole in the peanut head. Cut the neck to the desired length and cement the other end into the neck hole in the martynia pod body.

STEP 4. WINGS: Separate the two halves of the other martynia pod and trim off the claws. Trim the thick ends of the pod on a slant so each half will fit on the sides of the body near the neck. These are the wings. Cement them to the body using a small amount of cotton with the cement to help hold them to the body. If necessary, temporarily twist a fine wire around them to hold them in place while the cement is drying.

STEP 5. FEATURES: Fold the 2″ piece of leaf in half to make it a double thickness 1″ long. Cut a beak shape from this with the wide part of the beak on the fold. Put cement on the folded edge and slide it into the slit in the peanut. Cement two hemerocallis seeds in place for eyes.

STEP 6. PAINT AND BALANCE: Paint the entire bird white. When the paint is dry, paint the legs, eyes and beak black.

Adjust for balance by changing the bend in the knees and the spread of the toes until the bird will stand alone.

MARTYNIA DRAGON

Immature or closed pods are called for in making two creatures — the flamingo and the dragon. These pods are used because the claws have not yet opened out into two parts — thus one heavier curved line is formed.

The dragon is a must in any pod menagerie or zoo. It is simple to make and very little material other than the martynia pods is needed for it .

Materials Needed

3 martynia pods, 1 unopened
2 martynia seeds for eyes
Paint in a bright color; red, orange or green
Cement
Cotton

STEP 1. HEAD, BODY AND LEGS: Cement the stem end of one open pod, with claws coming forward, into the cleft between the claws of the other open pod. Claws of this pod also come forward. These are the dragon's legs.

STEP 2. MOUTH: To make his mouth, split the stem on the top pod from side to side and temporarily hold it open with a wedge until the mouth will remain open without it.

STEP 3. TAIL SECTION: The unopened pod will have only one claw. Cement the stem end of this pod into the cleft of the body pod with the claw going back and up to make the tip of his tail. Use cotton with the cement.

STEP 4. PAINT AND FEATURES: Paint the entire dragon and, when dry, cement the eyes in place. This dragon is painted a brilliant flame color, and is, naturally, very fierce!

MARTYNIA OWL

The owl is perched on a teasel stem that has the bracts still on it. The teasel itself has been removed. This is a wise-looking bird who knows that a pin may be fastened to his back so that he can be worn as a lapel pin.

Materials Needed

    1 martynia pod for head and body
    1 teasel stem and a small twig for perch
    2 artificial eyes or two squash or pumpkin seeds for eyes
    1 martynia seed for beak
    Cement

STEP 1. SHAPE OWL: About half an inch up from the cleft in the pod, cut the claws off. These stubs that are left on the pod are the tufts or ears on top of the owl's head. Since owls have short tail feathers, cut the stem off quite close to the pod (half-an-inch or less) to make his tail.

STEP 2. FEET: Use the sharp tips from the cutoff claws to make feet. Snip the tips about an inch long and cement them to the body so that the curved tips come forward to curl around the perch.

STEP 3. FEATURES AND PERCH: Cement eyes and beak in place. Cement feet to the small twig perch, which is then cemented in a horizontal position across the teasel bracts.

MARTYNIA FLAMINGO

Materials Needed

    2 martynia pods (one closed or immature) for body
    1 thevetia (yellow oleander) pod for head
    Small piece of dried cattail leaf for beak
    4 pieces, 18" long, #26 wire for legs, toes and neck
    Pink paint
    Black paint
    Cement
    Cotton

Plate 37. Martynia pod crane, dragon, owl and flamingo

Plate 38. Martynia pod deer

The flamingo is made in the same way as the crane with these exceptions: 1. For the body, clip the claws off the immature martynia pod and use the pod in an inverted position, that is, so that the short tail feathers of the flamingo will point down. 2. The wings, too, are placed in the same inverted position to follow the line of the body. 3. The head, which is turned to the rear, is a thevetia seed which has been slit vertically on its own natural line of division to hold the bluntly pointed cattail leaf beak. 4. Eyes are painted on and, of course, a flamingo is pink!

MARTYNIA DEER

A charming little deer can also be made from the martynia pods. Of course, many other creatures may be made after this same basic pattern simply by changing the size and shape of the head and the length of the tail. In selecting the two pods for the body of the deer, match them for size and slant of claws so that the legs will have maximum uniformity.

Materials Needed

3 medium-size martynia pods for body and neck
1 smaller martynia pod for antlers and head
2 hemerocallis seeds for eyes
1 red sandalwood seed for nose
3 tufts of hare's tail grass for ears and tail
Cement
Cotton
Brown paint
White paint

STEP 1. BODY AND LEGS: Trim the stem off and split one of the two pods you have matched for the body. Cement the halves halfway over the second pod, stem ends overlapping its stem end. Use cotton with the cement. The four claws curving down and toward each other will form the four legs. These legs may need to be shortened to achieve a natural look.

STEP 2. NECK: The third medium-size pod is the neck and part of the antlers. Snip the claws to two or three inches, turn them back and up, and cement the pod into the cleft between the front legs.

STEP 3. HEAD AND ANTLERS: Snip the stem closely off the small pod. Cement the pod in a horizontal position in the cleft of the neck pod, with its claws hooked under the claws of the neck pod. Its claws should curve up and forward. Arrange and trim both sets of claws to look like antlers.

STEP 4. PAINT: Paint the entire deer brown. When he is dry, paint a few white flecks on his hips and chest.

STEP 5. FEATURES: Cement the hemerocallis seed eyes one on each side toward the back of the head. Holes may be drilled to set the eyes in better position. Sand or cut the martynia pod at the nose to provide sufficient base for attaching the red sandalwood seed. Cement on grass for ears and tail.

Plate 39. Cattail dachshund

CATTAIL DACHSHUND

The cattail's naturally furry look makes a most realistic dachshund (Plate 39.)

Materials Needed

    1 very large diameter cattail for body
    1 large diameter cattail for head
    3 small diameter cattails for legs and ears
    2 medium day lily seeds for eyes
    1 large day lily seed for nose
    1 piece, 2″ long, twig, stem, or taped wire for tail

STEP 1. HEAD AND BODY: Cut the stems off both ends of the largest cattail and the rounded tip end will be the rear of the dachshund's body The head is a 2½″ to 3″ piece cut from the other large cattail; the rounded tip of this one to be the nose. To join the head to the body, cement the cut ends of the two cattails together so that the nose is raised.

STEP 2. LEGS AND TAIL: Cut two small cattails in half to make four legs 1½″ to 2″ long. Cement them in the desired position on the underside of the body so that the flat ends are on the table. Adjust the legs so the dog will stand balanced.

For the tail, cement the two inch piece of twig, stem, or taped wire to the tip end of the "body" cattail.

STEP 3. FEATURES AND EARS: For the nose, cement the large day lily seed to the tip of the head. Cement one small day lily seed to each side of his head in the proper place for eyes. To make his long, fuzzy ears, cut half of a small cattail in half lengthwise. Cement one piece to each side of his head with the rounded end pointing down and the fuzzy side showing.

GOLDENROD-STEM OSTRICH

Galls are very common where goldenrod grows. The ostrich described below was suggested by the single stem of goldenrod with two galls on it. The whole head, body and beak are just as picked, except for the tufts of feather (Plate 40.)

126

Plate 40. Goldenrod gall ostrich

Materials Needed

1 stem goldenrod with 2 galls on it for head, body and beak
Bits of teasel head for feathers
3 pieces, 9″ long, #22 wire for legs and feet
Green or brown Floratape
Black paint for eyes
Cement

STEP 1. FEATHERS: The goldenrod stem was picked leaving enough stem beyond the head gall for a beak. Snip two small tufts out of a teasel head and cement them on for the head and tail feathers.

STEP 2. LEGS AND FEET: Using a color of tape to harmonize with the color of the galls, tape the full length of the three 9″ wires individually. Cut the wires in half. Each leg will consist of three 4½″ taped wires, taped together starting one inch down from one end. Bend the one inch wire ends to form toes, two forward and one back. Drill two holes in the underside of the body and cement the legs into these holes. Bend the knees backward and arrange the legs and toes to enable the ostrich to stand alone.

PEANUT CREATURES

Children love these clever little animals, made from the readily available peanut. There is no limit to the different kinds you can make with a bit of imagination, some knowledge of animal forms, and enough peanuts. Just as no one ever eats only one peanut, no one stops at making only one peanut animal.

RABBIT

Materials Needed

Peanuts with shells on
Pipe cleaners
Duco cement
Seeds (sweet pea, radish or other for eyes)
Shellac or paints if desired (watercolor, tempera or ordinary wall paint)

Tools

> Large darning needle (for younger children, thread with bright wool
>   so it won't be lost)
> Shears or wire cutter—for cutting pipe cleaners

STEP 1. HEAD AND EARS: For each rabbit (Fig. 32), select two small round peanuts, one slightly larger than the other. With darning needle, make two holes for ears in smaller peanut. Have both holes come out together underneath to form a neck hole, (A). Insert one pipe cleaner through each hole, leaving 2″ at the top, (B); bend back to form ears as shown, (C).

STEP 2. BODY AND TAIL: Make a lengthwise hole in the larger peanut and push the neck pipe cleaners through the body and out; curl ends around to form ball for tail. (D).

STEP 3. LEGS: With darning needle make holes across the body for forelegs and hind legs. Push two pipe cleaners through these holes, (E), and bend to form paws and legs, (F). Snip off any extra length.

STEP 4. FINISH: Glue on seeds for eyes, or paint them on. Then paint your rabbit, if you wish, though he will be just as amusing in a natural peanut color.

Fig. 32. *Making peanut rabbit*

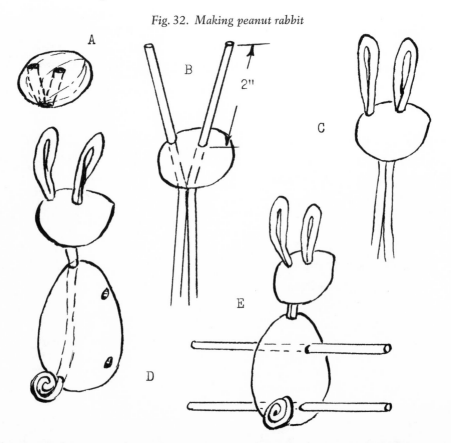

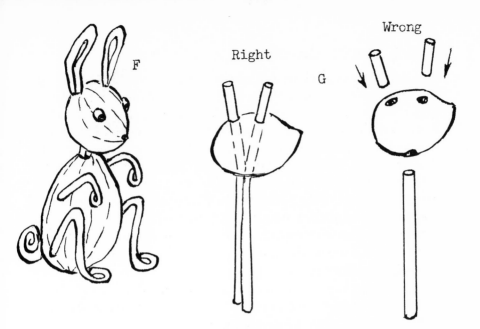

F

Right

G

Wrong

Fig. 33. Making parts for other animals

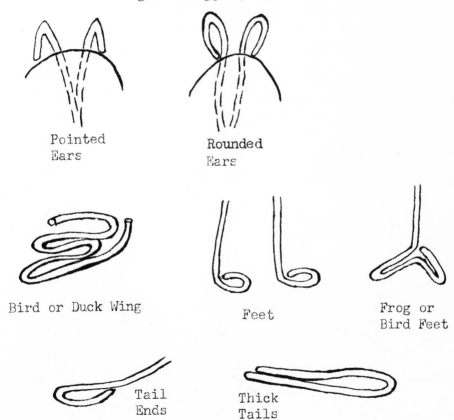

Pointed
Ears

Rounded
Ears

Bird or Duck Wing

Feet

Frog or
Bird Feet

Tail
Ends

Thick
Tails

129

OTHER PEANUT CREATURES

You can make enough peanut animals (Fig. 34.) to fill a zoo using the same materials and general directions as for the rabbit. When you start making the animals pictured here, you will soon discover that the peanuts themselves suggest many more animals and variations on the same animal than can be shown here. In fact, you may find yourself making animals that have never before been seen by human eyes.

HORNS OR EARS: Always have the "ear" pipe cleaners run through the peanut and out the neck hole, as you did with the rabbit; this strengthens the construction. *Do not* snip separate pieces for each part. To make the ears more pointed or more rounded, to suit the individual animal, see Fig. 33.

LEGS AND FEET: Follow directions as given for rabbit.

WHISKERS FOR CATS AND MICE: Draw several strands of darning cotton through the nose with a darning needle.

OTHER PIPE CLEANER DETAILS: See Fig. 33.

TO PRESERVE THE ANIMALS: Give them a coating of shellac, if they have been painted, the paint should be thoroughly dry before shellacking.

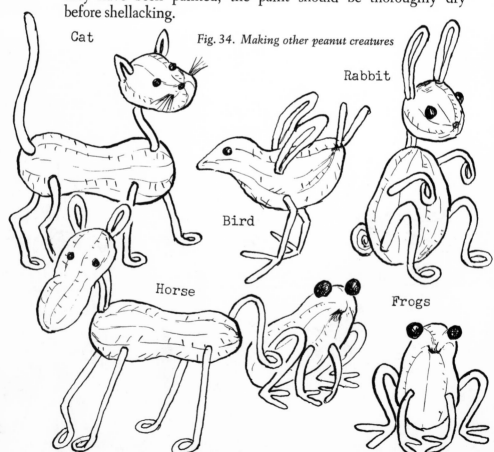

Cat

Rabbit

Fig. 34. *Making other peanut creatures*

Bird

Horse

Frogs

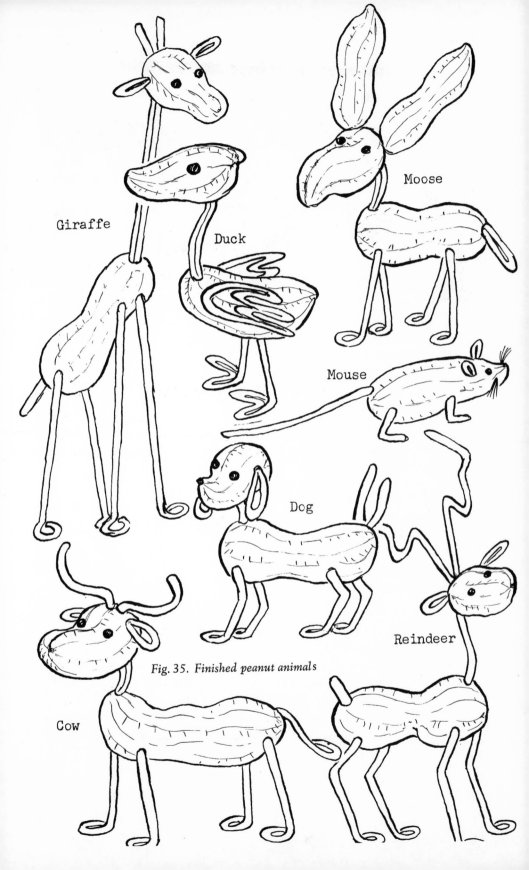

Giraffe

Duck

Moose

Mouse

Dog

Reindeer

Cow

Fig. 35. Finished peanut animals

Plate 41. Peanut animal mobile

PEANUT ANIMAL MOBILE

Although children are especially intrigued by them, people of all ages enjoy mobiles. Here are instructions for you to create a merry-go-round or circus using the peanut animals, (Plate 41, Fig. 35).

Materials Needed

> Dowel or strip of wood, 12" to 14" long or 3 cattail stems tied together with yarn
> 2 small colorful toy umbrellas, each about 9" in diameter
> Bits of colored yarn or a ball of variegated yarn
> Bright paint
> 2 small screw eyes

STEP 1: Paint the dowel that suspends the umbrellas. You may also paint the umbrella tips and handles to add more color to the mobile. Put aside to dry.

STEP 2: If the tips of the umbrellas are wood, you will be able to put a tiny screw eye into each one to make it easier to hang. At each rib tip of the umbrella, tie a peanut animal with colored yarn and hang it 2" or 3" down from the umbrella. Tie the yarn around either the neck or middle of the animal, whichever makes it hang straight.

STEP 3: When the animals are tied in position, tie each umbrella with colored yarn so that it hangs down about 3″ from the dowel and far enough apart so they won't bump into each other as they turn. Make a cord for the mobile to hang from by braiding together six long strands of yarn. Tie this around the center of the dowel and hang the mobile wherever you want it.

You can make the animals spin around by turning the umbrella handles in one direction until the yarn is twisted tightly. In effect, you wind it up. Then let go and the animals will whirl like a merry-go-round.

"Noah's Ark" variation: Use a toy boat and hang the animals in pairs from the sides in the same way as from the umbrellas.

FISHING BIRD

Materials Needed

> 2 martynia pods for body and wings
> 1 acorn for head
> 2 crabeye seeds for eyes
> cattail stem (small piece) for bill
> 2 tiny feathers for crest on head
> Pipe cleaners
> Brown Floratape
> 3 pieces, 18″ long, #18 wire, for neck and legs
> #30 or #32 wire for binding
> Cement and cotton
> Shellac

Fig. 36. Making fishing bird

STEP 1. PREPARE PODS (Fig. 36): Remove stems from both pods. These pods, when dry, separate into two points or claws at one end (*A*). For our bird's body, it is more useful to have only one heavier point (this will be the tail), so soak the pod in warm water for about 15 minutes until it becomes pliable. Then gently force the two points together and bind with fine wire (*B*). Let dry overnight. This is the body. Split another pod lengthwise into two parts; each of these parts will be used later as a wing for the bird.

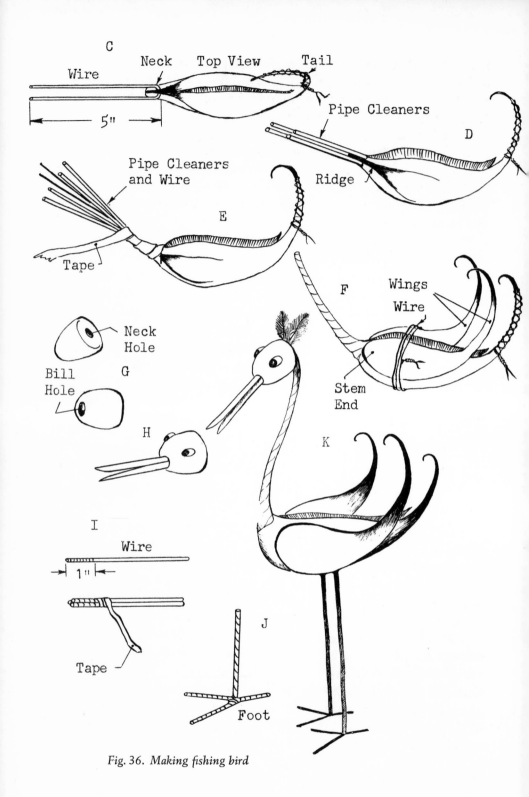

C — Wire — Neck — Top View — Tail — 5"

D — Pipe Cleaners — Ridge

E — Pipe Cleaners and Wire — Tape

F — Wings — Wire — Stem End

G — Neck Hole

Bill Hole

H

I — Wire — 1" — Tape

J — Foot

K

Fig. 36. Making fishing bird

STEP 2. ASSEMBLE BODY, WINGS AND NECK: When the pod with the wired-together tail is dry, pierce a hole through the ridge on top of the neck. Put a 10″ length of #18 wire through the hole and bend it in the middle so that each end is approximately 5″ long (C).

Next take four pipe cleaners and lay the ends of them beside the four ridges of the pod, letting them extend forward above and below the wire (D). With brown Floratape, bind the wires and pipe cleaners smoothly and firmly together, starting at the pod and working outward to the end of the wire (E). Clip off the extra length of pipe cleaners. This gives the bird a flexible neck that you can bend to any angle you choose.

Now take the two half-pods (the wings) and put a small piece of cotton saturated with cement into the stem end of each pod. Put more cement on the body (on each side of the stem end) and place the wings in position. Wrap fine wire around the body and wings to hold them in position until cement dries (F). Allow plenty of time to dry. Lay aside and go on to the next step.

STEP 3. HEAD: For the head, select an acorn about ¾″ in diameter without the cap. Make four holes in acorn. The first hole is made on the flat end where the cap was and must be large enough to securely hold the neck of the bird. (Note: to make holes in an acorn, hold an ice pick or darning needle in pliers over a gas flame, electric burner or even a candle. When heated, push the point quickly and firmly into the acorn and you have a hole very quickly.)

Make a second hole for the bill at the opposite end of the acorn (G). This should be a longer, more oval, hole. The bill may be made from any available twig or dowel or matchsticks. Cut two pieces about 2″ long, the one slightly shorter than the other and on a slant at the tip end. Put the two together as shown (H), and wedge and cement them into the hole for the bill.

The other two holes are for the bird's eyes. Make them large enough to hold a crabeye seed and cement seeds in place, black end of seed out. Lay head aside to dry.

STEP 4. LEGS: Legs should be as long as the neck but not as thick. Cut six 6″ lengths of #18 wire, three for each leg. Wrap 1″ of each with brown Floratape, (I), then wrap the three wires together, not wrapping over the taped part. Bend the individually wrapped wires out to form the toes, two to the front and one to the back, (*J*).

STEP 5. ASSEMBLE BIRD: When all the individual parts are dry, put cement into the neck hole of the acorn and force neck in. Shape the neck to a graceful curve. Remove wire from around wings and tail. Make two holes under the body for the legs. Put cement in the holes and wedge the legs in. Let dry at least 15 minutes.

STEP 6. FINISH: Shellac the whole bird and allow to dry overnight. When dry, cement two tiny feathers on the top of the head, and there is your bird! (*K*).

FISH

Another project that even the littlest children can help make. (Fig. 37.)

Materials Needed

> 3 small, unopened red pinecones (Scotch or turpentine may be used)
> 1 large, open pinecone (white pine or Norway spruce) for fins
> Piece of cornhusk for tail of 1 fish
> 6 crabeye seeds, for eyes
> Cement and cotton
> Sandpaper and shellac

STEP 1. BODY AND TAIL: We have used three fish in this mobile, (Fig. 37) so select three cones of different sizes, the longest one about 2″ long. Put a piece of sandpaper on the table and sand the large end of each cone at an angle on each side (*A*); this makes a plane for the eyes.

Slit the small end of the cone with a razor blade for the tail fin (*B*). Make tail from one or two scales from a larger cone or from a dried cornhusk cut to shape (*C*). Wedge a tiny piece of cotton soaked in cement into the slit to make the tail stay firmly in place. Cement the tails on all three fish and put aside to dry.

STEP 2. FINS AND EYES: Slit each cone for fins on the top and the two sides. These fins are made from large, single scales slightly trimmed to shape. Cornhusks may be used instead, although the top fin is better made from a pine scale, since it needs to be stronger to support the fish from the mobile. The fins are all cemented into the slits in the same way as the tail was (*D*). Let dry thoroughly.

136

Meanwhile, cut crabeye seeds in half with a razor blade to make eyes for the fish. (*Note:* These Seeds Are Poisonous When Broken, So Do Not Get Them Into Mouth, Eyes Or Open Cuts.) If you wish to avoid cutting the seeds, make holes in the cones and sink the seeds into them in the same way as for the bird's eyes (*E*). When fins are dry, cement eyes into position. When all parts are dry, shellac each fish and hang up to dry.

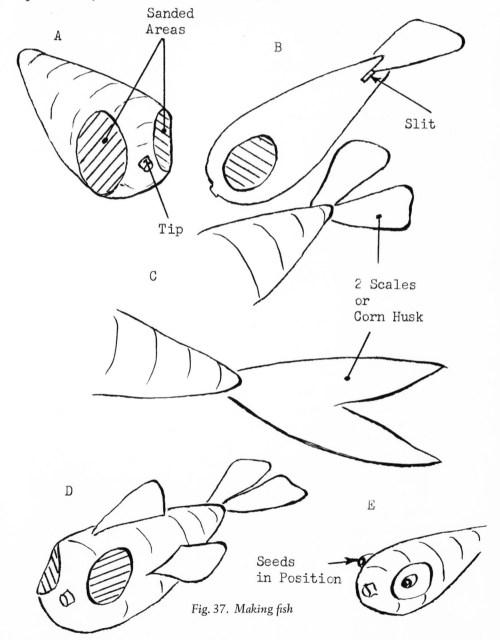

Fig. 37. *Making fish*

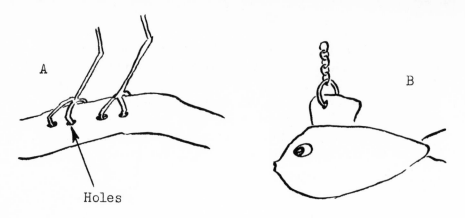

A

B

Holes

Fig. 38. Assembling fishing bird mobile

FISHING BIRD MOBILE

Hang over baby's crib, or anywhere in the house! (Figs. 38 and 39.)

Materials Needed

> 1 piece driftwood about 20" long
> Fine chain or strong thread
> 4 or 5 tiny screw eyes

STEP 1. FINISH DRIFTWOOD: If there are any unpleasantly rough spots on the driftwood, sand them smooth. Then either wax or shellac it and let dry.

STEP 2. PLACE BIRD: Hold the driftwood in the position in which you want it to hang. (You may save yourself a difficult balancing feat if you try first to see how the wood tends to hang naturally.) Then choose positions along it for the bird and the three fish. Place the bird in position and curl the feet around the wood at that point. Attach by making three holes in the wood for each foot so that you can curl the claws under and into the holes with pliers (A). Use cement around claws to strengthen. Bend its legs for a natural appearance. Bird's knees bend backwards. Turn the head to one side as if it is looking at the fish. (Birds look to the side, not forward.)

STEP 3. PLACE FISH: At each point where a fish is to hang, put in a tiny screw eye. With a hot darning needle, burn a small hole in the top fin of each fish. *Do not* pierce holes because the fins will split. Put a small wire link through the hole and attach a

138

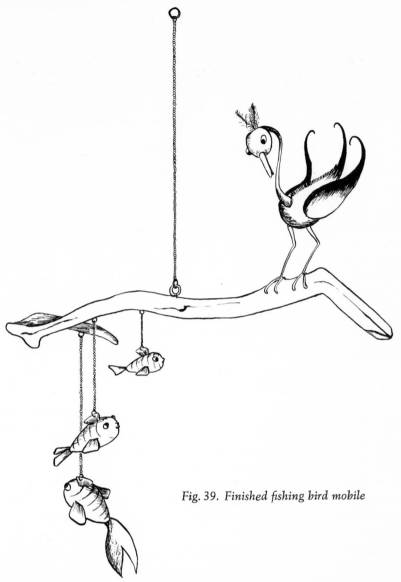

Fig. 39. Finished fishing bird mobile

fine chain to it (*B*). Cut the chain to the length desired and with another link attach it to the screw eye in the driftwood. Hang all three fish this way.

STEP 4. BALANCE MOBILE: Find the center of balance along the length of the driftwood. Put in a screw eye at this point on top, and attach the chain for suspending the mobile from the ceiling.

If the mobile tends to tilt slightly forward, suspend a fishing sinker from a strategic point to balance it.

139

5. STRANGE FLOWERS from NATURAL MATERIALS

HOW TO WIRE AND TAPE MATERIAL

There is a great deal of variation in the handling of wire and tape by individuals, which makes the difference between a fine piece of work and a slipshod one. At a flower show, poor workmanship or bad technique can cost you the blue ribbon. A good and original design can be a loser if bare wires or bulky, fat stems show.

The wire should be of the finest so that it will hold the material of your choice in position. Too fine a wire might not have the rigidity that is necessary, in which case, two fine wires are better than one heavy wire. Generally buy 18″ lengths of #30 or #32 wire, if you can find it, and cut them in half to make 9″ lengths for wiring stems. It is better to have the wires too long than to have to splice them. (Fig. 40.)

WIRING ITEMS WITH NATURAL STEMS

(Poppy seed pods, thistles, privet and most other leaves)

STEP 1. Since some natural stems are weak, tender, or brittle, and others are too smooth to be wired securely, it might be well to wrap a bit of Floratape twice around each stem before wiring it (A). But first pull and stretch the tape as far as you can before wrapping it around the stem (See *Taping*, Step 2); handle stem gently. This first bit of tape will serve as an anchor for the next tape that you put on, and will keep the wire from cutting through the tender natural stem.

STEP 2. Wind the middle of the wire two or three times around the stem on top of the tape, pulling it very tight and firm (B). The wire doesn't ordinarily need to be twisted more than once or twice since the next tape you put on will hold it securely. Do not overwrap with any wire, at most, three times around will be ample. The wire should be close to the piece being wired, and wrapped as tightly as possible around the stem. This is the secret of good technique.

140

STEP 3. Cut the natural stem to about one-half inch long; this is the bottom of the taped section (C).

STEP 4. Start taping the stem from right close under the piece being wired down to the end of the wire stem. This stem is usually four to six inches long, depending on its placement in the design (D).

STEP 5. If it becomes necessary to lengthen a wire stem, it will be most helpful to tape at least a part of each of the wires used before taping them together (E). This will hold them firmly together with no slipping around as bare wires are apt to do. The tape sticks to itself, which also prevents unfinished-looking, loose ends.

Fig. 40. *Wiring and taping*

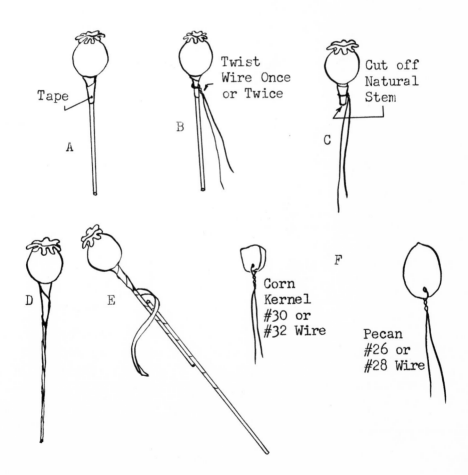

WIRING SOFT ITEMS WITHOUT STEMS

(Okra pods, corn cob slices, teasel slices, etc.)

STEP 1. For materials such as teasel slices (teasels cut into cross sections and, therefore, having no natural stem) and others with a soft center or hollow stem; cement a piece of pipe cleaner into the center or stem. Treat this pipe cleaner as if it were the natural stem.

STEP 2. Tape and wire the pipe cleaner stem and trim it to the half-inch length as above (C). For most corsage items, the pipe cleaner is too heavy and bulky to be used for the full length of the stem.

WIRING HARD ITEMS WITHOUT STEMS

(Nuts, seeds, pits, closed cones, etc.)

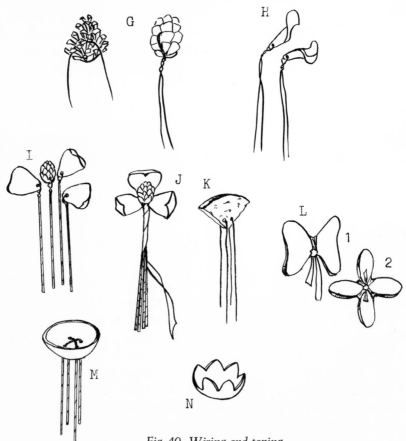

Fig. 40. Wiring and taping

STEP 1. To wire a seed, nut or any hard item that doesn't have a stem, you must make a hole for the wire through the base of the piece. Some of the less woody items such as corn kernels, melon or pumpkin seeds can be pierced with a darning needle. Harder items such as pecans, Brazil-nuts and pinecones can easily be drilled with a small electric drill.

STEP 2. After drilling the hole, pull a wire through it and twist it two or three times to hold the nut or seed securely (F). The weight of the wire is determined by the delicacy or toughness of the material being wired. For a corn kernel or melon seed, a #30 or #32 wire would be strong enough to hold it without cutting through it, while a #26 or #28 wire would be necessary for a heavier and tougher item such as a pecan or a pinecone.

STEP 3. When the wire is in place, tape it as in (D).

WIRING PINECONES

As with any other item being wired, the thickness of the wire to be used is determined by the weight of the cone. For a tiny light cone such as the hemlock, a #32 wire is adequate.

STEP 1. Push the wire between the scales two or three rows up from the stem end of the cone. Pull it halfway around the cone.

STEP 2. Then pull it tightly into the core of the cone and down to the stem end where it is twisted firmly two or three twists to become a wire stem (G).

STEP 3. Tape it as in (D).

TAPING

Tight, adequate wiring and smooth slender stems, the result of careful taping; that is what you're striving for.

STEP 1. MAKE TAPE NARROWER: Floratape comes in many colors, the most useful of which are green and brown. If your wire stem is very slender, it would be a good idea to cut the tape in half, making two lengths, each one-fourth inch wide. Narrow tape gives a smoother, thinner stem. The cutting can be done by laying a few inches of tape on a cutting board or piece of cardboard, then slicing the tape in half lengthwise with a razor blade. Shears can be used, but the razor is faster and easier. Some of the ladies in this area, whose technique is as near perfection as possible, cut the tape into thirds. This does take more time and effort to cover the wires with so narrow a strip of tape, but the result is beautiful.

STEP 2. STRETCH TAPE: The tape will stretch to almost double its length. Do stretch it to its utmost length to make a thinner covering. The tape may break at first, which does no harm, but soon you will have the feel of it, and your reward will be stems that are excellent in technique.

Materials needed are not specified in each project. The following applies to all projects in this chapter. Quantity will be determined by the number of flowers you wish to make. Wire, floral tape and cement are needed in all crafted flowers in this chapter.

PINECONE FLOWERS

A large variety of flower forms may be crafted from pinecones. You may use scales individually wired and assembled to make two, three, four or multi-petaled flowers. Or you may use part of a cone, (a cone slice, tip, or end) as a flower. Here are a few interesting examples. (Plate 42 and Fig. 40.)

PINYON SCALE SNAPDRAGON

Each snapdragon is made from two small center scales of the pinyon cone, matched for size, wired and taped separately then taped together.

HEMLOCK CONE VIOLETS

The hemlock cone is a tiny cone and each violet uses one cone. Just twist the center scales out of the tip of the cone and wire it Tape the stem and then assemble finished violets into flower clusters if you wish.

WHITE PINE SCALES WITH BUTTERNUT CENTER

This somewhat larger flower, 2½" to 3" across, uses seven white pinecone scales, wired and taped individually. A butternut cut in half, wired and taped, is the center. Arrange the petals evenly around the center and tape together.

PINYON SCALES WITH NORWAY SPRUCE CONE TIP CENTER

Make the same as *White Pine Scales with Butternut Center.*

Plate 42. Pinecone flowers: A. Pinyon scale snapdragon; B. Hemlock cone violets; C. White pine scales with butternut center; D. Pinyon scales with Norway spruce cone tip center; E. Pinyon scales with hemlock cone cluster center; F. Pinyon cone, tip end; G. Deodar cone; H. Pinyon cone, stem end

PINYON SCALES WITH HEMLOCK CONE
CLUSTER CENTER

The reverse side of four pinyon scales and a cluster of six hemlock cones make this flower. Each separate item is wired and taped before assembling.

PINYON CONE TIP END

Unusual because of its green color; it is a rather short cone and either end can be used as a flower. Wire it the same as any cone and snip a few scales out of the tip if necessary.

145

DEODAR CONE

The beautiful deodar "rose" cone usually must be purchased, and will probably already have a short pipe cleaner stem cemented in when it comes to you.

PINYON CONE STEM END

See instructions for *Pinyon Cone Tip End.* Your cone flowers will be varying shades of brown, except for the pinyon. Their color can be enhanced and their life extended by giving them a coat of shellac. For more cone flowers see chapter VI, (Plate 50).

BASIC PETALED FLOWER WITH CENTER

Most multi-petaled flowers are put together in the same way. Individually wire and tape each unit of the flower (See: Wiring and Taping, in the beginning of this chapter) Arrange the petals around the center, and tape all the stems smoothly together. Fig. 40 (*H*), (*I*) and (*J*).

Examples of flowers made this way are shown in Plate 43 using these materials: peanut shucks, party rye bread, orange peels, and potato slices.

ONION SKIN FLOWER

PREPARING ONION SKINS

To obtain onion skins, cut across the onion, making two halves. Very carefully remove the fleshy part of the onion, leaving the skin intact. Depending on the type of onion, you may get two skins from each half, though usually there is only one.

Put the skins in a saucepan, cover with hot water and add a tablespoon or two of glycerine. Place over *low* heat for about an hour. *Do not boil.* Remove from water and drain on newspaper or paper towels, then let dry for a day or two.

STEP 1. Wire a hemlock cone for a center (See: *Wiring and Taping*, (G). Slide the wire stem down through the hole in the prepared onion skin. A bit of cement on the base of the cone will hold the cone and onion skin together.

STEP 2. Tape the stem from right under the flower down to the end of the wire. Use pinking shears to give an interesting line to the edge of the skin. You have made a single flower.

STEP 3. If you want to make a double, put a second smaller skin inside the large one and put together as for the single flower.

146

For a fuller flower, wrap a piece of onion skin loosely around the cone center and tape the bottom part of the skin onto the wire stem. Then slide the wire stem down through the holes of two or three more skins. The more skins you add, one on the other, the more complex will be your flower. Skin edges can be turned back instead of pinked to make a finished look; see Plate 43 (B).

PARTY RYE BREAD FLOWER

Here is a somewhat less than ordinary use for any ordinary loaf of rye bread! But it must be fresh; stale bread will crack or be too bulky for a good flower form. Party rye bread is the loaf that is about 2½" in diameter and about 10" long.

STEP 1. Cut a slice of bread into quarters. Make as many quarters as you need petals for your flower. While the bread is still soft, pull two fine (#32) wires through the point of each quarter slice and bend all four ends down very carefully, taking care not to tear the bread. Do not twist the wires (See *Wiring*, (K)). Lay aside for a day or two until the bread is hard.

STEP 2. Gently twist the four wires together under each petal and tape them for an inch. Select a suitable center for the flower, (in this case we chose a willow gall), and wire and tape it (See *Wiring and Taping*.) When all the petals and the center are wired and taped, dip quickly in shellac and hang by wires to dry. If the shellac is at all thick, it may be best to make a solution of two parts shellac to one part shellac thinner (which is usually alcohol). This makes waterproof flowers so you don't have to worry about being caught in the rain.

STEP 3. Assemble the three, four, or five petals around the center to resemble a flower and tape all wires together to the end of the stem.

SQUARE LOAF WHITE BREAD FLOWER

STEP 1. Gather each square slice of bread carefully through the middle, keeping it flat on the table. When the center is only about 1" across, tie it in position with a half-inch wide strip of cloth. Now gather the slice from the opposite direction and tie it, too, in position. (See *How to Wire and Tape, beginning of this chapter.*) Lay aside to dry.

STEP 2. Select an appropriate center, wire and tape it. When bread is dry, remove cloth strips from the slice, brush thoroughly with shellac and let dry again.

STEP 3. Carefully pierce a hole in the center of the slice and pull the wired center down snug and tight to the middle of the bread. A bit of cement on the underside of the center will help to hold it there. Hang the flower, head down, for the cement to dry.

ROUND LOAF WHITE BREAD FLOWER

STEP 1. Gather two round slices of bread carefully once through the middle and tie each with a strip of cloth the same as for the square loaf above. Let Dry

STEP 2. Select center for flower; wire and tape it. When the two slices of bread are dry, remove the cloth strips, brush with shellac and let dry overnight.

STEP 3. Put the flower together by laying one slice crisscross on top of the other. Carefully pierce or drill a hole down through the center of both slices and slide the wire stem of the flower center down through the hole. A small bit of cement under the center will help hold it in place. Hang it upside down to dry. For an example of this flower, see the large focal flower in Plate 54.

SQUARE LOAF WHITE BREAD CALLA LILY

STEP 1. Trim the crust from the fresh square slice that is to be made into a calla lily. Select an appropriate center, a slim cattail or a butterfly-weed pod, and wire and tape it.

STEP 2. Roll the slice of bread around the cattail spadix, keeping one corner point at the top of the flower. Bring the sides around until the corners overlap in the middle; then wrap tape around the base of the lily and twist a piece of #28 wire snugly around on top of the tape. Wrap the bottom half of the lily with cloth strips to keep it in the desired shape and hang it upside down to dry.

STEP 3. When dry, remove the cloth strips, brush the lily with shellac, and another flower is born!

ORANGE PEEL FLOWER

STEP 1. Cut each half of the cleaned orange peel into six equal wedge-shaped pieces, cutting from the outer edge into the center. Using either a sharp knife or shears, cut each piece into a petal shape and, while it is still moist, pierce a hole in each petal about ½″ in from one point Fig. 40 (L-1). Lay petals aside on newspapers to dry, but do not pile them on top of each other. During the approximately two weeks they are drying, check and shape them daily.

STEP 2. Select a center for the flower; the center for the lower flower shown in (L-2), is lily leek (*Allium Moly*) the upper flower center is sections from the ostrich fern spore case. The orange peel flowers in the chapter on *Arrangements* show the effective use of this material for flower centers. Use about eight pieces for each center; tape all eight ends together, wire them, and tape the stem (See Wiring and Taping).

STEP 3. When the petals are dry, assemble them into a flower (See Basic Petaled Flower in this chapter). To make a bud, wire and tape two petals facing each other. Fig. 40 (*M*) and (*N*) shows detail of a grapefruit peel flower.

Plate 43. Ten strange flowers: A. Peanut shuck flower; B. Onion skin rose; C. Party rye bread flower; D. Orange peel flower; E. Grapefruit rind rose; F. Potato flower; G. Potato flower; H. Beet rose; I. Potato flower; J. Turnip slice calla lily

PREPARING GRAPEFRUIT RIND

You can make thickly-textured roses from grapefruit rind if you find the right grapefruit: one with a very thick rind.

STEP 1. With a vegetable peeler, remove all of the yellow part of the rind. Cut the grapefruit in half; then carefully remove all membranes and pulp from the inside. Cut each half into six equal pie-shaped sections.

STEP 2. Lay each section, in turn, flat on the table, and holding it firmly with an even pressure, slice it horizontally with a sharp knife to make two thin slices, each one half as thick as the original. You will have twelve, very thin slices from each half grapefruit. Trim them, removing any extra thick spots, so that each slice is of uniform thickness. Make sure that all colored rind is removed and that all you have left is the soft pulpy white inner-part of the rind. You will need at least a dozen slices for a gardenia and nearly twice that number for a rose.

STEP 3. Lay about four paper towels flat in the bottom of a shoe box or one of similar size. Sift in one inch of borax-cornmeal mixture, i.e. 2/3 cornmeal to 1/3 borax (see *Borax-Cornmeal Preserving,* Section II in Chapter I.), and spread the slices on this; they should lie flat and not touch each other. Next, cover these with one-inch of the mixture and place another layer of slices on top. Continue in this way until all slices are covered. Put the box in a dry place for about a week or until the slices are dry and crisp.

STEP 4. Remove from the cornmeal mixture and let the slices "rest" for a few days. They may be put on a tray or in a box, but be sure to cover them with a clean cloth to keep the dust out. To prepare them for the next step, brush each slice with a soft clean brush to remove all of the cornmeal mixture.

STEP 5. Make a solution of one cup of hot water (not more than 160°) and one tablespoon of glycerine, as much as you will need to cover the grapefruit slices completely. Mix solution with a spoon and put the brushed slices into it. Make sure that each slice is covered by the liquid. Let them stand for at least 24 but not more than 30 hours.

STEP 6. Remove the slices from the glycerine solution and place them flat on a clean cloth or on paper towels. They will be ready for use in about two days when they may be stored in cardboard boxes until needed. Each slice should be at least 2½" long.

GRAPEFRUIT RIND FLOWER

STEP 1. Cut grapefruit in half, remove all pulp and membranes down to the white inner part of the peel. Pierce four holes in the bottom near the center for two wires to be put in when it is dry. (See Fig. 40 *M* and *N*.) Drying will take about two weeks, and during that time, keep shaping the peel round every day or so.

STEP 2. Tape two pieces of #28 wire, and when the grapefruit peel is dry, pull the ends of the wire down through the pierced holes so that the two wires cross inside the peel, (M). Carefully twist the four wires together two or three times, and tape them. The centers for the single flowers in *Plate 57*, are seed heads of the *Allium moly*, cemented in place.

STEP 3. The more dense centers used in the petaled flowers (same arrangement) are bits of swamp grass, first painted the desired color and then cemented in place. Make the petaled grapefruit flower in the same way as the single one described, with these exceptions:

a. Use two half-grapefruit peels instead of one.

b. After the peels are cleaned and while they are still moist, use shears to cut five or six petal shapes part way down the peel (N). Do *not* cut the petals apart.

c. When it is time to wire stems to the flowers, set one petaled half inside the other and turn so that all the petals show before wiring them together.

POTATO FLOWER

STEP 1. Select a long potato with a round cross-section about two inches in diameter. Cut into slices ¼″ thick or less.

STEP 2. Spread slices on paper towels on a cookie sheet and place in oven at 150° to 200°. Watch carefully to keep them from getting dark brown; a light tan color is the goal. When the desired color has been reached, turn off the oven. Let them finish drying in the oven and keep checking so that they don't get darker as they slowly cool down to room temperature. Petals treated this way will be quite thin and translucent.

STEP 3. Variations may be made in petal shapes by cutting the potato into a square or three-sided cross section before slicing. Variations in color and texture may be made by the following methods:

FLOWER VARIATIONS

Clorox helps maintain light color. As soon as the slices have been cut, place them in a Clorox solution (one part water to two parts

Clorox). Let stand for several hours. The length of time will vary for different potatoes, so no definite time can be given. When the slices look very white and feel quite spongy, remove from the Clorox and dry with paper towels. Then proceed to oven-dry them as above.

Natural drying produces an opaque grey color. When the slices are cut, pierce them near the edge, slip a wire through (do not twist the wires together till dry) and hang up to dry. Potatoes dry in one or two days.

A *lemon juice dip* before drying will produce another soft effect. *Pour on boiling water* and let stand for five minutes, then drain and dry. Dry in salt.

Use a hotter oven — a variation in heat will change the degree of translucence, and also the length of time in the oven. The potato slice dries hard and inflexible, making it very difficult to pierce a hole for wiring. Of course, a hole may be pierced before the slices are dried, but the hole will shrink as the potato shrinks in drying. A small electric drill is very helpful when the hole must be put in after the slice has dried.

STEP 1. To make a single slice potato flower (Plate 43 (*I*), wire and tape the center to be used. With a needle or corsage pin, pierce a hole in the center of a fresh slice of potato, pull the wire stem of the center through the hole and hang it head down to dry. If the slices have been dried first, use a drill to make the hole for the center wire, as piercing will cause the slice to break. When dry, cement the center to the slice if necessary, hang upside down until cement is dry, and tape the stem. (See Wiring and Taping.) Each slice is a flower.

STEP 2. To make the five-petaled flower shown in Plate 43 (*F*), cut the potato slices in a triangular shape before drying them. Using a butterprint pod for a center, make a petaled flower. Some other suitable centers are hemlock cones, swamp buttons, grey sage heads, groupings of bittersweet berries or hydrangea blossoms.

STEP 3. A multi-petaled potato flower, (see chapter on *Corsages*), may be made if the slices are small enough. Wire several slices near one edge of the slice and arrange them around a wired center. The center should be larger than one used for a single slice flower.

DRIED VEGETABLE SLICE FLOWER

The origin of these flowers will be unsuspected by their admirers. Slices from any vegetables may be used, especially roots, beets, butternut squash, horseradish roots, turnips (rutabagas), and osage oranges may all be prepared this way. Finished flowers are shown in Plate 43.

PREPARING VEGETABLE SLICES FOR FLOWERS

STEP 1. Slice the vegetable into ¼" cross-section slices with the peel left on. Each slice when dried and shrunk will be used as one petal of a flower. A change may be made in the shape of the petals by cutting the vegetable into a square or triangle before slicing it.

STEP 2. Spread the slices out to dry on a flat surface that has been covered by a clean absorbent cloth. A cloth is usually better than newspapers because the newsprint comes off on some of the lighter colored items. When preservation of the natural color is important, keep the slices in a darkened place while drying, as light tends to fade colors. Drying may take two weeks or more. To insure maximum flexibility, daily pull and stretch each petal gently, first one way and then another, handling carefully so they will not tear. When dry, they will still retain some of their flexibility and may be pierced with a needle for wiring.

TURNIP CALLA LILY

STEP 1. Cut a dried turnip slice to a modified heart shape. Wire a slender cattail, cut 2" long, for the center or spadix. (See Wiring and Taping.)

STEP 2. Wrap the turnip slice firmly around the bottom of the cattail, the pointed part of the slice at the top of the lily. Lap one side over the other at the bottom and tape securely at the base of the flower. Wrap a piece of wire around on top of the tape, twist it, then tape the whole stem. See Plate 43 (J).

TEASEL CENTER FLOWER

These flowers are such fun to make! Cut the tip end off a teasel for a center (about an inch thick) and wire and tape it. (See *Wiring and Taping*, Fig. 40). Plate 43 shows teasel centers made from flat teasel slices as well as from the rounded tip end. Select the material you will use for petals; cone scales, seeds, sections of seedpods, etc. Put a little dab of cement on the end of each petal and push them one by one into the bottom of the teasel slice, in a ring around the center.

Plate 44. Teasel lily

TEASEL LILY

When the teasel seed heads have been weathered after maturity, they may be used to make a flower form that resembles a lily. Using a pointed knife, split the seed head from blossom end to stem, carefully so the sections will not break. Spacing it evenly, slit down the seed head six times around, making six petals, still joined at the bottom. Cement a small cone or seed into the center of the sections to hold the "petals" in an open position. (Plate 44.)

PHILODENDRON-AND-CATTAIL CALLA LILY

To make this lily, the philodendron leaves must be prepared about a week ahead of time. (See Chapter 1, Section III. *Glycerinizing by brushing.*)

Step 1. Cut a slender brown cattail to the length you will need for the spadix (center) of the calla lily. Wire and tape it.

Step 2. Curl a *prepared* philodendron leaf around the cattail,

154

pointed end of leaf up. Lap the bottom sides one over the other, wrap tape twice around to hold, and continue taping down the length of the stem. (See finished flower, Plate 45.) There is another picture in Chapter VI, *Arrangements*, showing the calla lily (Plate 52).

Plate 45. *Philodendron-and-cattail calla lily*

LUNARIA SCALE FLOWER

Prepare as many lunaria scales as you will need at least a day or two before you use them. (See: Chapter I, Section III *Glycerinizing by Absorption and Transpiration* and IX *Preparing ferns and lunaria*.) You will also need a small cluster of tansy or some other suitable material for the center of each flower and a poppy pod as a backing for the petals. (Plate 45). The lunaria is quite fragile, and care must be taken in handling it.

STEP 1. Cement five lunaria scales together to form a circle with a minimum opening in the center. Use a pin curl clip to hold the scales where they overlap while the cement is drying.

STEP 2. Wire the tansy center (See: *Wiring and Taping*) and tape the stem for about 2". Prepare the poppy pod by slicing off the top, or button, with a razor blade. Slice off all of the stem, then pierce a hole in the stem end of the pod.

155

STEP 3. Pull the wire stem on the tansy down through the opening in the lunaria scale circle and then through the poppy pod, stem end down. Put a bit of cement around the top edges of the poppy pod and pull it up snugly against the back of the flower. Hang it, head down, to dry.

ROSES

"A rose is a rose is a rose" — but not always; it may be a grapefruit rind, or a cornhusk, or some other unlikely material, when you are making your own. Roses made from several different materials are illustrated here, and though the material is different, the technique and manner of putting a rose together is essentially the same: *Grapefruit Rind Rose,* in Plate 43(E). *Beet Rose,* in Plate 43(H). *Butternut Squash Rose.* (See also Fig. 41 and 42.) These three roses are grouped together because similarity of the body and texture of the dried slices calls for the same techniques in handling the material. For grapefruit rind rose, first see Preparing Grapefruit Rind, earlier in this chapter. For beet or butternut squash rose, see Preparing Slices of Vegetables and Dried Vegetable Slice Flower, in this chapter.

STEP 1. Make a bud center as follows, using slices that are imperfect in shape, thickness or size; one slice rolled tightly forms the center. Wrap three or four slices closely around it, overlapping each one with the next as you wrap. Hold the slices in place by wrapping white thread around the bottom part of the roll. Pull the thread tight enough to hold the slices firmly in place, but not so tight as to cut through them. Binding at the bottom will also help the petals to spread out slightly at the top of the roll. Now put this bud aside while you curl the other petals.

STEP 2. Curl the corners of the top of each slice by rolling them over a pencil or knitting needle. Arrange each curled slice around the bud center, binding them at the bottom with thread, as necessary, until the rose is as large as desired. Keep pinching the bottom part firmly together to make it as compact as possible. When all the petals are in place, wrap tape several times around the roll at the bottom to cover the white thread. Cut off excess grapefruit rind or other material just under the tape, which should leave a thick, half-inch long stem under the rose.

STEP 3. Tape three 18″ lengths of #24 wire. Pierce straight through the taped stem at the base of the rose and pull one wire through. Do this with the other two wires, crisscrossing them

156

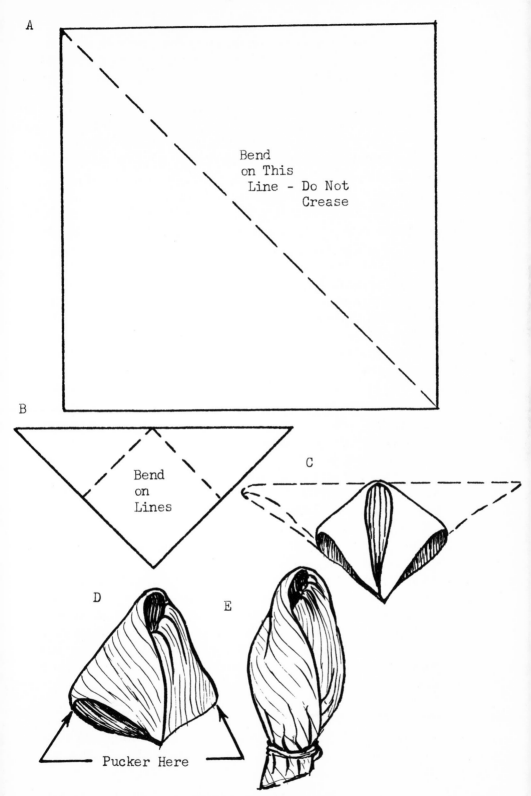

A

Bend
on This
Line - Do Not
Crease

B

Bend
on
Lines

C

D

E

Pucker Here

Fig. 41. Making a rosebud or rose center

under the middle of the rose, then bending all six ends down to form the stem, (see Fig. 40 (*J*). *Do not* twist the wires together; hold· them by taping them together for an inch or two. Start taping for the stem at the base of the petals and continue down the wire, adding one or two leaves as you go. (Directions for making rose leaves will follow). The length of the stem will be about ·9″, and it may be cut shorter or lengthened with more wires as needed.

CORNHUSK ROSE

Cornhusks should be permitted to dry completely after being removed from the ear; this may take several weeks. Field or feed corn has the better husks, and there is a variety that has husks naturally colored a beautiful pink to dark red. Use these to make a most realistic red rose, or, if you prefer, cornhusks may be dyed any color you choose by using fabric dyes. (Plate 46.)

STEP 1. When you are ready to make the rose, put two cups of hot water and two tablespoons of glycerine into a vessel (a bread pan is fine for this); then lay the cornhusks in this solution for about 15 to 20 minutes. Remove from solution and wrap in a towel. When most of the moisture has been absorbed by the towel, cut petal shapes out of the husks. The shape should be very much like the shape of a piece of pie, and all the petals will be approximately the same length from the tip of the pie-shape to the back, about three inches. The width of the petals across the back of the pie-shape, however, should vary from 1½″ to 2½″, the wider ones being used towards the outside of the rose. Cut the petals so that the grain of the cornhusk runs up and down (from the tip of the pie shape to the back). After they are cut, keep them in the damp towel till needed.

STEP 2. Now make the center of your rose. (See Fig. 41.) Select a large husk and cut it so you have about a 4″ square. Fold this in half so it makes a triangle; then curl the two top points down to the bottom middle point and, holding the points together, pucker the whole bottom area together to make a little hollowed-out bud shape. Wind with thread at the bottom to hold it and then lay it aside.

STEP 3. The next step is to curl the corners of the petals, and if you happen to be the proud possessor of an old electric curling iron, this can be accomplished very simply. Sort out the petals that have been in the towel and, taking the smaller ones first, use

158

Plate 46. Cornhusk rose and leaves

your curling iron to curl both corners on the wide edge of each petal. Roll the corner around the iron and hold long enough to get a natural-looking curl.

If you don't have a curling iron, use your electric iron set on the "rayon" setting as follows: Press each petal, and before it is completely dry, curl each corner on the wide edge over a ¼″ diameter knitting needle. Slide the needle out, pin the curl with a bobby pin or pincurl clip, and let it dry.

STEP 4. Proceed by either method till you have 12 or 18 petals curled. Starting with the smaller petals first, wrap them one by one around the bud center. To hold them, wind thread around the base of the flower as you place the petals around the center. When the rose is as large as you wish, break off the thread and wrap the base with Floratape. Wrap the tape at least three times around, keeping it close to the base of the rose.

STEP 5. To make the stem, wrap a piece of #28 wire twice around the taped area, pulling it very tight. Twist the wire together (three twists) to hold it; then trim off all cornhusk ends below the taped area. Add another #28 wire in the same way and pull down all four ends; tape down the length of them for a stem.

159

POINTS TO REMEMBER: When assembling the cornhusk or grapefruit rind rose, be sure to keep the thread at the same level as you add the petals. Gather the petals slightly around the bottom for an open rose, and lay them flat around the bottom for a less open flower. Also, the petals are placed a little higher as the rose gets larger.

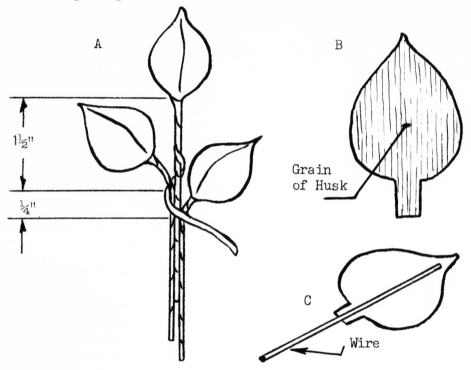

Fig. 42. *Making leaves for roses*

ROSE LEAVES

When you have finished making a rose, you may find that you will want rose leaves to complete the illusion. It would seem that the simplest solution would be to dry some real rose leaves, but trial and error methods have shown that real rose leaves are too brittle when dry and crumble very readily. A heavier-bodied leaf is required, and one of the best for this purpose is the privet leaf, which is very common and fairly small. It is oval in shape and one to one-and-a-half inches long by three-fourths of an inch wide. When you press and dry these leaves (See Chapter I, Section IV, on *Pressing*) leave a short stem on each one. Since a rose leaf is a multiple leaf, you will need three privet leaves for each rose leaf you make.

PRIVET LEAF ROSE LEAVES

STEP 1. Tape and wire (#32 wire) each dried privet leaf as described in Wiring.

STEP 2. Assemble the rose leaf by placing one leaf at the top and another leaf about an inch-and-one-half below it. Tape the two stems together and tape in the third leaf stem about one-fourth inch below the second. See Fig. 42(A). Continue wrapping to the end of the wire stem.

CORNHUSK ROSE LEAVES

For the cornhusk rose, color and texture patterns may be better carried out by making the leaves, too, from cornhusks.

STEP 1. Using the pattern in Fig. 42(B), cut six leaf-shapes out of cornhusks for each rose leaf you wish to make. The grain should run up and down.

STEP 2. Place one cornhusk leaf-shape on the table and cement a piece of #30 covered wire down through the center, extending several inches below the leaf, Fig. 42 (C). Then cement another leaf-shape exactly on top of it to cover the wire. Make sure the edges match, or trim them when the cement is dry. Make three of these wired cornhusk leaves.

STEP 3. When dry, assemble them into a rose leaf in the same manner as the privet rose leaf.

GRAPE CLUSTERS

Pecans and hickory nuts (Plate 47 and 48)
Candlenuts and butternuts (Plate 49)
Acorns, kidney beans, hickory nuts

Custom build your own artificial grape clusters to achieve exactly the texture, color, shape or size desired for the arrangement or other decoration you are making. Pecans, filberts, hickory nuts and horse chestnuts, wired or tied and grouped together, make as effective a bunch of "grapes" as any you can buy. Try walnuts, black walnuts, or even Brazil nuts. Butternuts and candlenuts will give an unusual texture, and kidney beans or acorns make smaller grapes. Almonds are too brittle unless the hard-shelled ones are used. Any of these nut "grape" clusters may be painted with flat or glossy paint, dusted with silver or gold glitter or used in the natural state; depending on the effect you wish. They will be much more of a conversation piece than the usual plastic grapes.

STEP 1. To make a bunch of grapes, you will need from 20 to 40 nuts, depending on their size and the size of the cluster desired. Drill a small hole in one end of each nut. Apply a drop of cement over the hole and insert one end of a six inch length of covered wire into the hole. Use plenty of cement and be sure that the wire goes at least one-half inch into the nut. Allow the cement to dry for 24 hours.

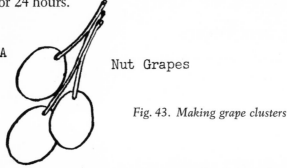

Nut Grapes

Fig. 43. *Making grape clusters*

If, for some reason, you cannot drill the holes; there is another method you may use. Cut a small square of either plastic wrap or discarded nylon stockings. Wrap the nut smoothly inside the square bringing all edges together at the bottom of the nut. Wrap a #32 wire tightly around, cut off the excess and tape the wire stem. The plastic wrap gives a shiny, very protective covering for the nut, while the stocking will give a slight color change.

STEP 2. Tape the nut stems into clusters of three, Fig. 43(A), with no two nuts at exactly the same level.

STEP 3. When all the nuts are in clusters of three, start taping the clusters together. Starting at the tip of the bunch of grapes, tape one cluster to another. Work gradually up the stem, adding one group at a time. When the bunch of grapes is of the desired size, tape all the wires together to make the stem. Bend and shape it to a natural position.

STEP 4. Spray entire cluster with clear plastic or paint or finish as desired.

Plate 47. Bleached hickory nut "grapes"   *Plate 48. Bleached pecan "grapes"*

BLEACHING NUTS FOR GRAPE CLUSTERS

The grape clusters shown in Plate 47 were made from small pecans and hickory nuts that were bleached before using, in order to achieve a lovely soft-white color. If the hickory nuts are found soon after dropping from the tree, they will already have a very nice white color, but if they have lain on the ground and weathered for some time, the color will be a rather dirty grey. It will not take as long to restore the white color to the hickory nuts as to remove the darker color from the pecans.

Either one may be soaked in a strong bleach solution as follows: Use a glass or plastic bowl, or any container that won't rust, since rust will discolor whatever you're bleaching. The container should be large enough to hold all the nuts and the solution. When you put the nuts in the water, they will float to the top, and if they are not completely immersed they will have a mottled color. Therefore, use an inverted saucer on top of them to hold them under the solution as they soak.

Check for color every 15 minutes. If the solution is strong enough and they soak long enough, they will bleach to a lovely off-white color. Sometimes it is necessary to soak them for several hours to get the desired whiteness. When the color is achieved, rinse them and let dry thoroughly, perhaps for a week. Better just practice the virtue of patience and wait. If you use the oven to dry them, the oil inside the nut may seep through and discolor or darken the shell.

Plate 49. Candlenuts, and butternuts "grapes"

6. DRIED ARRANGEMENTS

There are no more satisfactory flower arrangements than those composed of dried plant material. There are three potent arguments in their favor: They are beautiful and a joy to create. They are long-lasting and require little upkeep. They are economical of time, effort and money.

A well-planned and artistically designed dried arrangement will be as beautiful as an arrangement of fresh material. No effort has been made to elaborate on design or color, although a working knowledge of both is necessary for dried and fresh arrangements alike. The advantage, however, lies with the dried arrangement. You may start today and take as long as you wish to create it; no harm is done if you take it apart time after time to obtain the desired effect. I have had arrangements in the making for weeks, only to take them apart and start all over again. The use of dried material gives you time to think of and consider every placement. It gives you time to study the various principles and elements of design since you need not worry about flowers and foliage wilting.

A fresh arrangement may take several hours to compose and, at the most, will last only a few days. The arrangement made of dried subjects may take as long to make, but will last for years if reasonable care is used in handling. If made of more sturdy material, your arrangement may quite often be washed by laying or standing it in the bathtub and using a fine spray from the shower. After it is dry, it will look fresh and new again. A light spraying or brushing with white shellac before assembling into an arrangement will help to preserve and waterproof your material. If carefully done, the shellac will bring out hidden colors and will add life and a soft glow to the over-all picture.

Certainly you will also learn good mechanics, since it is sometimes difficult to anchor thin stems and hide the various means used for support without the aid of the fresh pliable materials used in the fresh compositions. Sometimes a 1″ or 2″ length of cattail stem (fresh or dry) wired to the bottom of a wire stem will enable you to keep the material in place in a needlepoint holder.

In using fresh plant material you are governed to a great extent by its form, color, and natural length of stem. This is much less true when using it in its dried state since stems are all wired and can be shaped and extended as needed to give absolute control of the material's position in the arrangement.

I also seldom use props such as figurines or other items not classed as plant material. They may be used if you wish, but it is my contention that there is so much of everything in nature that very little, if any, artificial material is needed to create a striking and unusual decorative unit.

Some of the arrangements that follow are described in a general way; that is, I have not given the exact number of stems, flowers or leaves required. Plant materials vary so much in size and form that it would be difficult to duplicate most arrangements exactly. The purpose of showing these arrangements is to stimulate your interest in this wonderful world of dried plant material. We are also hopeful that they will assist you in working out ideas for your own use and pleasure.

SIX TIPS FOR EASIER DESIGNING

Most people find it difficult to achieve good design in an arrangement. As in all of the other arts, familiarity with one's medium is the best way to get a finished product that will have the elements and principles necessary for a work of art.

Reading many books will give you a broader understanding of flower arranging or the crafting of flower forms out of dried plant materials for home or flower show, but here are six steps that may be helpful:

1. Determine where the finished decoration will be placed: on a dining or coffee table, in a hall, on the TV or on the piano, etc. This will govern the size and shape of the arrangement.

2. What will be the color of the background or neighboring objects? This determines the colors used.

3. Choose the container. The color, size and shape of the container is plainly indicated by the size and shape of the space it is to fill, and the background colors.

4. Choose the flowers. Having followed steps one through three, limitations of size and color of the plant materials has been established, also, the amount that may be used to best advantage.

5. Make sure that your mechanical aids such as holders, lead strips, oasis, styrofoam or others are adequate and secured properly so there will be no tipping or slipping of stems to throw the design off balance.

6. Arrange the decoration at the same height as it will be, when placed in its permanent position. If it is on a low table, it should be made so that it will look well on all sides and from the top. If on a mantle, where one has to look up to view it, then special attention should be given to the lower part.

Plate 50. A. Sensitive fern; B. Royal fern; C. Nigella; D. Lycopodium candles; E. Annual poppy pods; F. Ostrich Fern; G. Red pinecone tip; H. Willow galls; I. Red pinecone stem end; J. White pinecone, cut in half crosswise; K. Lunaria with wire stem; L. Lunaria with natural stem; M. Outer scales of lunaria; N. Three hemerocallis seedpods; O. One iris pod; P. A "flower" made from four apricot pits with Australian pinecone center; Q. Another apricot pit "flower" with a burr oak center; R. Larch cone with tip removed; S. "Rose" from Norway spruce cone cut crosswise; T. "Rose" from pinecone cut crosswise

At home, any or all of the materials may be treated, dyed, painted or glittered. For a flower show, read the schedule to see whether any one or all of these are permitted.

When making an arrangement for a show, the schedule for that show should be carefully studied and followed. However, when the arrangement is made for home use, there are no restrictions except those of good taste. It is true that beauty is in the eye of the beholder, and not all tastes are alike, but good taste in decoration speaks a universal language.

SOME EASILY AVAILABLE MATERIALS

Easily available materials particularly useful for dried arrangements are pictured in Plate 50. All but the fern spore cases and one lunaria stem have been shellacked, wired, and taped.

Plate 51. Palm spathe and driftwood

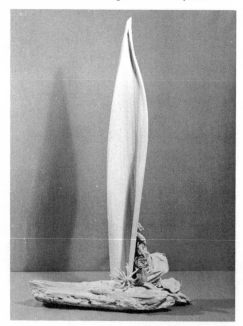

PALM SPATHE AND DRIFTWOOD ARRANGEMENT

An old piece of driftwood with a palm spathe screwed to the back of it is the base of this decoration. A florists' water pick is cemented to the back of the spathe on the right side in case fresh material is used. A dozen small to medium deodar roses, two bunya-bunya scales and a traveller's palm seedpod are used to decorate the right side. A spider eucalyptus pod is a little to the front of the other pods. The entire unit was sprayed several times with flat white paint (Plate 51.)

LUNARIA SCALE FLOWERS AND PHILODENDRON CALLA LILIES

Here is a most ethereal and fragile-looking creation. Each blossom was made of five white lunaria or money plant scales and each calla lily is a philodendron leaf with a slender cattail spadix. The alabaster container resting on a marble slab makes the final result fit to grace the most elegant surroundings. (Plate 52.)

Materials Needed

> 5 lunaria scales (inner), for each flower
> 6 lunaria scales (outer), for each leaf
> Sprays of tansy, for flower centers
> Grapevine tendrils
> Poppy pods, for calyxes and buds
> Philodendron leaves (var. *cordatum*), for calla lilies
> Slender cattails, for calla lily spadix
> #26 wire, fine-covered wire #30-32, and #18 wire
> Brown floral tape, cement
> Clear plastic spray

STEP 1. Make about 24 lunaria scale flowers (See Chapter V, *Strange Flowers.*)

STEP 2. Make six leaves using the outer tan lunaria scales. Cement two outer scales together with a 4″ piece of covered wire between them. Hold together with a pincurl clip while cement is drying. It will take three of these for each leaf. Tape the three wire stems together into a single leaf unit. You will need approximately six of these leaf units.

STEP 3. Make philodendron and cattail calla lilies (See Chapter V, *Strange Flowers*).

STEP 4. Wire about eight grapevine tendrils and four or five poppy pod buds with #26 wire, and tape stems for about 2″.

Plate 52. Lunaria scale flowers and philodendron calla lilies

STEP 5. Take an 18″ length of #22 wire and start assembling the tall spray by taping the smallest poppy seedpod and a tendril at one end of the wire. Tape each new unit to the wire continuing smoothly down to the end of the stem, adding flowers, leaves and tendrils as you work. Add heavier wire where needed for greater length and strength. One large and four small sprays were assembled.

STEP 6. Fill the container with sand (or, a piece of styrofoam wedged into the container will do) and insert the wire stems of the lunaria flower sprays and the philodendron calla lilies in the desired positions.

STEP 7. Spray entire arrangement with clear plastic.

170

LITTLE BROWN JUG—ALBIZZIA PODS

"Little brown jug how I love thee" — Some of the most appealing arrangements have been done using brown jugs! This one has color changes of bronzy-green and tan that do not show in the picture, but tie in beautifully with the natural colors of the rather commonplace materials used. Plate 53.

Materials Needed

Florida fern
Candlenut leaves (sycamore leaves are a good substitute)
Albizzia pods
Willow galls

Two Florida ferns, dried without pressing, are the highest placement. They are a soft grey-green color. Two candlenut leaves are placed next, one pointing up and the other down. They too, are a soft grey-green color. Albizzia pods in a bronzy-green color are placed next, some pointing up and some down, leading the eye to a cluster of velvet-soft, grey-green willow galls.

Two wood staging blocks of a soft matching color are placed under the container.

The whole presents a quiet, restful picture in subdued colors to make a simple, effective arrangement.

Plate 53. Little brown jug—albizzia pods

BREAD ARRANGEMENT

A lovely metal container and a praying figurine were the inspiration for this arrangement made entirely of slices of sandwich bread. The bread must be *fresh*; stale bread will crack or be too bulky for a good flower form. Plate 54.

Materials Needed

Bread slices from a square loaf, for small flowers, calla lilies and leaves
Bread slices from a round loaf, for large flower
Arborvitae cones (6 for each flower), for centers
6 butterfly weed pods or 6 slender cattails about 3" long, for spadix for calla lilies
1 willow gall, for round flower center
12-18 stems of bearded wheat
Strips of cloth ½" wide for tying
#32, #28 and #18 wire
Tape and cement
Gold paint

Plate 54. Bread arrangement

172

STEP 1. Make as many flowers as you need, each flower uses one slice from a square loaf of bread and six arborvitae cones for a center. (See chapter V, *Strange Flowers, Party Rye Bread Flower.*) The arrangement pictured uses from eight to twelve square slice breadflowers. Make one or two extras in case of breakage.

STEP 2. Make leaves also using square slices. Tie the slices to shape them exactly as for the flowers, but when they are dry, use a sharp knife to cut each slice into 4″ petals. Three such petals make one leaf. Pierce two holes about ½″ in from the pointed end and draw two taped #28 wires through them, one in each hole. (See Strange Flowers — Wiring and Taping). Bring the four ends down and tape together for about 2″. Then tape them together in units of three to make each leaf as shown in arrangement.

STEP 3. Make larger flower from round slices of bread and a willow gall center.

STEP 4. Make calla lilies. The 6 used here have butterfly weed pod centers.

STEP 5. Assemble flowers and leaves into groups. Starting at the top of an 18″ length of #18 wire, tape the wire stems of the smaller leaves or flowers to it. Add more leaves and flowers as you work down, but three or four flowers and one or two leaves are the most for any one section. The six calla lilies are made into two groups.

Place three or four wheat stems in a group, the stems not more than 6″ long and no two stems exactly the same length. Tape the bottoms of the stems together. Wire over the tape using #22 wire and then tape the wire stems. Where greater length and strength are needed, tape in #18 wires. (See *Strange Flowers, Wiring and Taping.*)

STEP 6. Spray each group with a different value of gold paint. This includes the wheat groups as well as the container and figurine. The ·darker values should be at the bottom of the arrangement. When gilding, variation of gold tones eliminates any possible monotony of color values.

STEP 7. Assemble the groups into a rather formal design. The calla lily groups are at the left and bottom. Start at the top with the wheat groupings and place them at different levels along the left side down to the lower calla lily.

TEASEL BRACT FLOWER ARRANGEMENT

A delightful arrangement can be made using teasel bract flowers. Plate 55(A).

Material Needed

> 10 to 12 teasels

STEP 1. At the base of every teasel is a light airy arrangement of long, curling, spiny bracts. By removing the teasel just above these bracts, an interesting flower is obtained.

Remove it using heavy shears to cut off about 1" of the tip; then snip off several slices about ½" thick until you have only the bracts and a little of teasel left. This end will be the teasel bract flower; and the tips and ½" slices can be given wire stems to make flowers without the curlicues or they may be used to make another kind of teasel flower. (see: *Strange Flowers.*)

STEP 2. Give each teasel flower a wire stem (see: *Strange Flowers, Wiring and Taping*), then tape flowers together into two or more groups and arrange groups in container.

If the teasels are green and fresh, the color will be a lovely, silvery green when they are dry.

SPENT THISTLE FLOWER ARRANGEMENT

As a companion piece, the arrangement at the right, Plate 55 (B), is composed of spent thistle blossoms. If the thistles are gathered before they have been exposed to much weathering, they, too, will have a lovely soft silvery sheen. Tan and creamy in color, they are delightfully airy and graceful.

Material Needed

> 10 to 12 thistle flowers

STEP 1. Pull the fuzzy centers off and brush the thistle to groom it. Remove any dead or loose petals. Cut the stems to about ½" long.

STEP 2. Give each flower a wire stem (see: *Strange Flowers, Wiring and Taping*). Tape into sprays, arranging blossoms at different levels, and arrange in container to make a pleasant airy arrangement.

174

Plate 55. Teasel bract flowers and spent thistle flowers

ORANGE PEEL FLOWER ARRANGEMENT

Dried orange and grapefruit peel may be made into some very delightful long-lasting flowers. The size of the finished flower will depend on the size orange or grapefruit from which the peel was taken. Plate 56.

Materials Needed

> Peel from 3 or 4 oranges
> 5 or 6 glycerinized ligustrum leaves (See: Chapter I, Section III, *Glycerinizing.*)

STEP 1. For this arrangement, make six orange peel flowers and three buds. (See: Strange Flowers.)

STEP 2. Wire each ligustrum leaf. (See Strange Flowers, Wiring and Taping.)

STEP 3. Assemble all units into one main stem, adding the rich brown ligustrum leaves at the bottom. The oriental ginger jar is filled with clean bird gravel and set on a black teakwood stand. Anchor the spray of orange peel flowers in the gravel. This is an excellent means of holding stems just where you want them while giving weight to the container.

Plate 56. Orange peel flower arrangement   *Plate 57. Grapefruit peel lotus arrangement*

GROUPING OF GRAPEFRUIT PEEL LOTUS

Grapefruit rind lotus flowers are, indeed, an attention getter. Plate 57.

Materials Needed

> Peel from 2 or 3 grapefruit
> 5 or 6 glycerinized ligustrum leaves (See Chapter I, Section III, *Glycerinizing.*)

STEP 1. Make five grapefruit peel lotus flowers. (See: *Strange Flowers, Grapefruit Rind Flower.*)

STEP 2. Wire each ligustrum leaf. (See *Strange Flowers, Wiring and Taping.*)

STEP 3. Assemble. (See *Strange Flowers, Orange Peel flower.*)

176

SQUASH CONTAINERS

Many seedpods or vessels can be fashioned into useful and interesting containers. The summer or crookneck squash is one of the most versatile items and makes ideal cornucopias either in an upright or horizontal position. Any of the gourds may be made into containers to be used with a wide variety of fresh or dried plant materials. Plate 58. Do not cut the gourds or squash before they have cured and are completely dry. This drying may take six months. To prepare summer squash for use, see *Crafty Critters, Summer Squash Creatures.*

Materials Needed

> 1 summer (crookneck) squash, for cornucopia
> 1 slice agave stem, for base
> Cement and cotton
> Shellac
> Paraffin, for waterproofing inside of squash

STEP 1. After the dried squash has been dampened to make it less brittle for cutting, use a fine-toothed saw to remove a 2″ to 3″ thick slice from the large (or blossom) end of the squash. Remove seeds and other dried particles from inside the squash. Allow squash to dry thoroughly again, perhaps for two more days.
STEP 2. Use the slice from the bottom end to hold the squash in the vertical or horizontal position that you choose. Cement the two pieces together using a small amount of cotton to help the cement to hold, and then prop in the desired position until the cement has set.
STEP 3. Waterproof the inside. An easy way to have wax always ready is to save all old candle ends, paraffin, and bits of wax in an old coffee pot. Then when you need it, place the pot in a wide shallow pan of hot water to melt it. Wax should never be melted over direct heat.

Plate 58. Squash containers

Plate 59. Cholla cactus root container and coconut container

Pour about ½ cup into the upright section and swirl it around so the entire inner surface is covered. This application of wax should be quite hot so that it will penetrate the shell of the squash. Do not allow any wax to spatter on the outside as it will prevent shellac or paint from adhering. When this wax has hardened, pour another ½ cup of wax inside, not as hot as the first, and swirl to coat again. Enough wax should remain in the bottom to make a level base inside for a needlepoint holder. The squash container may now be used for fresh plant material as well as for dried.

STEP 4. Cement the container onto a slab of the agave blossom stem or on any other type of base. The agave is eminently suitable in color, texture and form.

STEP 5. Shellac for natural color, or paint if any other color is desired.

DOUBLE CORNUCOPIA SQUASH CONTAINERS

For the double cornucopia, two squash are needed. The process is the same as for the single cornucopia except that both are glued to a single squash slice base, and to each other. No other base is needed as the container should stand by itself. Plate 58.

CHOLLA CACTUS ROOT CONTAINER

Cholla cactus roots are not easy to find. If you are fortunate enough to get one, saw, whittle or sand the bottom of the root so that it will stand solidly without any teetering. Sand the root to obtain a smooth surface, and brush to remove all loose particles. Then give it a coat of shellac, or several coats of paste floor wax,

178

buffing or brushing after each coat. A small glass or tin can, inserted inside the container, will hold water if fresh plant material is used. Plate 59.

COCONUT CONTAINER

If you can get a coconut in the husk which is somewhat longer than round, and suitably colored, it can be made into a handsome container by simply sawing a slice off the stem end.

After sawing, remove the meat from the nut inside, and allow the husk with nutshell still inside to dry thoroughly.

Cement the sawed-off piece to the bottom of the coconut in an inverted position using a little cotton saturated with cement to make a firmer bond. The container shown is decorated, at the point where the two pieces join, with dried sections of the pandanus fruit; although any small cones, nuts or other seeds or pods can be used. Plate 59.

Wax or shellac for a finished look after all cement is dry.

For information about bases for dried arrangements see chapter I, section XI, *Holding Driftwood in Position.*

HOLIDAY DOOR CORSAGES

Door "corsages" are such gay and inviting decorations. This one was planned for Christmas but you can make them for any season and quite often add a pleasant touch to any event. Try one for your next party or for a holiday occasion. Plate 60.

SUMMER SQUASH BELLS AND TINSEL BEADS

Materials Needed

> 4 dried summer squash (cut in half and use only the stem ends)
> 12 tinsel bead stems (on wire) 8" or 9" long
> 8 tinsel bead stems (on wire) 12" long
> 2 yds. ribbon
> #18 wire
> Tape and cement
> White paint
> Note: Before cutting squash see Crafty Critters, Summer Squash Creatures.

Plate 60. Door corsage of summer squash bells and tinsel beads

STEP 1. If squash have stems, remove them by sawing off close to the squash. Then saw the squash in half crosswise, remembering that the stem-end half should be long enough to make a convincing bell. Remove the seed mass, but leave the fibrous inside part close to the shell to add interest and texture. Make a hole straight through the stem end of each squash bell. With heavy, sharp shears, cut about six scallops into the edge of each shell. Snip slowly and carefully to avoid cracks since the shell is quite brittle.

STEP 2. Paint the cut edge and the outside of each bell white, and let dry.

STEP 3. Make a center for each bell by taping three of the shorter tinsel bead stems together for the full length of the wire stem. Bring the taped wire through the hole in the squash, and put a generous dab of cement over the hole to hold the wire in place. Put centers in the other bells and let cement dry.

STEP 4. The long tinsel bead stems are used as background in the corsage. Tape them together as for the centers in the following

180

way; one group of three, two groups of two each, and one single taped stem.

STEP 5. Arrange the four bells and tape the stems for an inch to hold them together. Add the tinsel stem groups in the background and the white satin bow to complete the effect.

GILDED SUMMER SQUASH AND FIELD CORN

A variation on the summer squash bells is shown here. The corn and the squash bells have been gilded and red Christmas tree ball clappers pick up the red of the huge satin bow. Used as is, or set on a big wreath of evergreens, this is a striking and unique bit of door decor. Plate 61.

Materials Needed

      3 dried summer squash (cut in half and use only the stem ends)
      3 red Christmas balls for clappers
      5 or 6 dried ears of corn
      3 or more yds. of satin ribbon
      #18 wire
      Tape
      Gold spray or paint

STEP 1. Make three squash bells the same as for the preceding project (Bells with Tinsel Beads), but do *not* scallop the edges.

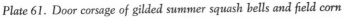

Plate 61. Door corsage of gilded summer squash bells and field corn

STEP 2. Wire the ears of corn by twisting a wire tightly around the ear and down between the kernels near the stem end of the ear. (See *Strange Flowers, How to Wire and Tape*.)

STEP 3. Gild the ears of corn and the squash bells and hang to dry.

STEP 4. Attach each Christmas ball to a wire stem, then make a taped wire stem for each squash bell by bending a loop on one end of the wire, and pulling it up through the hole in the stem end of the squash so that the loop will be inside. Attach the wire stem of the Christmas ball clapper to this loop, measuring to make sure the clapper is hanging in the right position.

STEP 5. Arrange the three bells and tape their stems together. Add the ears of corn, taping in the stems one at a time. Add big red bow at top.

HOLIDAY PLAQUES

"WEDGWOOD" GRAPEFRUIT PEEL FLOWER

An old picture frame with a cardboard backing is the background for this gentle bit of wall decor done entirely in Wedgwood blue with touches of silver. Plate 62.

Plate 62. Plaque of Wedgwood blue grapefruit peel flowers

Plate 63. Silvery moon wreath with orange peel flowers

Materials Needed

Grapefruit rind for flower
Monkey face eucalyptus for center
6 mahogany pod petals for flower
Grey sage head for center
5 ligustrum leaves
6 sensitive fern spore cases
32 cone grass stems
2 eucalyptus clusters

STEP 1. Make grapefruit rind flower. Make mahogany petal flower. (See: *Strange Flowers, Basic Petaled Flower.*)

STEP 2. Spray all materials wedgwood blue except the cone grass stems and the eucalyptus clusters which are to be sprayed with silver. This includes the frame and the cardboard background. When the blue is dry on the frame, silver the beading on the inner edge of it.

STEP 3. Using bits of wire, fasten all materials to the cardboard background in desired position.

SILVERY MOON WITH ORANGE PEEL FLOWERS

A round wire wreath frame was cut and reshaped to make the crescent moon form for this hanging ornament. Plate 63.

183

Plate 64. Artichoke candle holders and mantel decoration

Materials Needed

> 5 orange peel flowers
> Ostrich fern spore cases for centers
> Blue paint
> Silver glitter

STEP 1. Wrap the moon form with white Floratape. Then carefully wrap it again with 1″ wide (or narrower) blue satin ribbon. The tape underneath prevents the ribbon covering from slipping.
STEP 2. Make the orange peel flowers (see *Strange Flowers*) and assemble into a spray.
STEP 3. Spray the flowers with light blue paint, and then glitter them and the center section of the crescent with silver glitter.
STEP 4. Check for balance and attach a loop of ribbon on upper section of crescent for hanging.

**ARTICHOKE CANDLE HOLDERS AND
MANTEL DECORATION**

Dried artichokes in a metallic green against a flat black background makes the plaque with matching candlesticks for a dramatic mantel decoration at Christmas. Plate 64.

Materials Needed

    8 dried artichokes of various sizes
    2' x 3' plywood panel
    Flat black paint
    Metallic green paint

STEP 1. Paint the plywood panel with flat black paint. It may take two coats to get good coverage. Allow to dry thoroughly and be very careful in handling it as flat black surfaces show even the smallest mark.

STEP 2. Choose six artichokes with some natural stem left on them. (These may be purchased already dried from any shop which is a source of dried materials.) Arrange them on the panel in the design you wish. It may be necessary to remove some of the scales on the back to make the artichoke stay where you want it.

STEP 3. Spray or paint all the artichokes with metallic green paint and let dry before attaching to the background with cement or wire, or both.

STEP 4. For the candlesticks, use 2 artichokes of similar size and shape. Remove all the stem and enough petals to make them sit squarely. Either cut or pull out enough of the center so a candle can be placed upright in the hole.

STEP 5. Paint these the same metallic green and give the lightest touch of the same color to white candles.

Plate 65. Maple seed insects with strawflower

MAPLE SEED INSECTS WITH STRAWFLOWER

Dragonfly, moth and flies imaginatively created from winged seeds are the subject matter of this eye-catching bit of wall decor suitable for a holiday gift for a nature lover. Plate 65.

Materials Needed

> 4 hard-maple seeds for dragonfly wings
> 1 eucalyptus pod (or twig) for dragonfly body
> 1 clove, for dragonfly head
> 2 soft-maple seeds, for moth wings
> 1 seed part only of maple key, for moth body
> 2 hairs from a clematis seed pod for moth antennae
> 4 mountain maple seeds, for flies
> 1 strawflower
> Running pine, foliage
> Background: Cardboard painted or covered with cloth or construction paper

Each piece is cemented separately to the background. For example, the dragonfly's wings are cemented down first, and then the body and head cemented in position.

Maple keys or seeds vary in size and shape so do collect an assortment before you start this plaque.

TEASEL TREE

Here is a do-it-yourself Christmas tree with an inverted 5″ flowerpot base, both sprayed in a metallic green, to add a most effective touch at Christmas. Plate 66.

Materials Needed

> 50 to 60 teasels (graduated sizes) for tree
> 5″ flowerpot, for base
> #18 wire
> Floratape
> Metallic green paint

STEP 1. The teasels must be graded and matched for size with the smaller ones to be used at the top. Cut off all except 1″ of each teasel stem. Put a drop of glue over the hole in the remaining stem and push a 9″ long piece of #18 wire up into the teasel. Tape the entire stem, starting immediately under the teasel head. Wire and tape about 50 teasels in this fashion, keeping sizes together in groups of five.

186

STEP 2. Start assembling the tree using a medium-size teasel in an upright position at the top. Arrange five of the smallest teasels evenly around this and tape all stems together. The wire stems will have to be bent to set the teasels at the proper angle.

Add another row of five small teasels under and between the first row. Tape these stems to the first group of stems. Continue in this manner using successively larger teasels as you go down. Our tree has ten rows from top to bottom not counting the tip. Tape each five wires to the main stem as they are added. All wires are caught in a single thick stem several inches long when the tree is completed.

STEP 3. Place a piece of hollow stem, such as bamboo, bocconia, sunflower, or Japanese bamboo inside the flower pot around the hole and hold or secure it in an upright position. Fill the pot with melted wax or plaster, which, when hard, holds the hollow stem firmly to provide a tube to hold the wire stem of the tree. (The wax may have to be poured a little at a time and allowed to harden before pouring the next small amount. This will prevent it from running out the small hole in the bottom of the pot.)

STEP 4. Spray whole unit metallic green or any color chosen. This tree will last indefinitely.

Plate 66. Teasel Christmas tree

7. CORSAGES, HATS and JEWELRY

GENERAL INFORMATION ON CORSAGE TECHNIQUES

Conversational corsages, yours for the making! So novel are the materials that you'll have everyone trying to guess what you have used. Again, our suggestions are not the only possibilities. You may well use some "finds" of your own. The following are some reminders on technique and some notes on the treatment of the more unusual materials.

1. Use your imagination and your eyes to find suitable and interesting material.
2. Use only perfect, clean items.
3. Use good taste and good principles of design in combining colors and forms.
4. Don't crowd your materials. Leave some voids for interest.
5. Wire every flower, leaf, tendril or stem that is used in the corsage with the appropriate size wire. Remove all but about ½" of the plant stem and use a wire in its place.
6. Wrap all wire stems neatly and smoothly with a harmonizing color of Floratape. If Floratape is unobtainable, a half-inch strip of crepe paper in the correct color may be used, but it will not hold as well as the tape.
7. Where stems are of very fine wire, cut the Floratape in half lengthwise to avoid making too bulky a stem.
8. Learn to make neat bows. Loops need not be exactly alike, but should not be too dissimilar, either.
9. Wire bow separately and add it after the corsage is completed. Then if you wish to change bows, it will take only a second and can be done without disturbing the design.
10. Place your corsage in a covered box or in a corsage bag when it is not being worn. You would not leave a fresh corsage lying around to gather dust, so give some care to your dried corsage and it will last longer.

SOME SUITABLE CORSAGE MATERIALS

Most corsage material is necessarily small, therefore easily overlooked. Once you know what you're looking for, dry plant material for corsages is surprisingly easy to find, perhaps right at your fingertips. Below is an extensive list of suitable materials, but it by no means exhausts the endless possibilities, which are limited only by your own inventiveness.

Cones

Arborvitae
Blue Spruce
Chinese fir
Deodar
Hemlock
Larch
Mugho pine
Norway spruce
Pinyon pine
Red pine
Scotch pine
Sugar pine
White pine
White spruce

Fruit Pits

Apricot
Date
Peach
Plum
Prune

Seed Cases

Baptisia
Bee balm
Beech-nut burrs
Echinops
Eucalyptus
Gladiolus
Hemerocallis
Lily
Mock orange

Morning glory
Nigella
Poppy (annual)
Queen's crape myrtle
Radish
Rose hips
Sea oats
Sweet gum
Sycamore

Leaves

Cecropia
Eleagnus
Podocarpus
Privet
Silverleaf

Seeds

Cardamon
Chinaberry
Corn
   Calico
   Finger
   Squaw
Ear-pod
Hubbard squash
Job's tears
Kidney beans
Melon
Palm
Sandalwood
Sea-bean
Watermelon

Miscellaneous

Bread
Cattails (slender)
Fern spore cases
Grapefruit rind
Grasses—all kinds
Kapok blossom calyxes
Lycopodium
Pampas and plume
   grass
Pine needles
Pussy willows
Willow galls

Vegetables

Beets
Corn—husks, leaves,
   cobs
Horseradish root
Onion skins
Potatoes
Squash
   Summer
   Butternut
Turnips

Nuts

Acorns
Beech-nuts
Hickory
Horse chestnut
Italian chestnut
Peanuts

ASSEMBLING AND "DRESSING UP" THE CORSAGE

When all of the units of your corsage are wired and taped, assemble them into a pleasing design. Try, at least at first, to stay within a specific design form such as the triangle, the oval, the round, the crescent, or the Hogarth line. When you have the units in their best possible position, wrap a bit of tape around all stems to hold them in place. Do not twist the wires together, and do not twist another wire around to hold the stems. Two or three times around with the tape will hold everything securely. Clip the corsage stem to be no more than one to two inches long, and bend it to follow the line of the design.

Backing and Ribbon

To add extra glamour to your corsage, you may set it against a nylon net backing; or you may want to add a touch of color or texture by using ribbon points or tiny nylon net fluffs. The color will be indicated by the materials used and the costume on which it will be worn.

NYLON NET BACKING: To make an average size backing you will need a half yard of nylon net about 5″ wide. Fold this net strip in half lengthwise. Using a piece of #28 wire as if it were a needle, thread it into the fold for the length of the strip, gathering the strip together as you go. Gather it as tightly as you can and twist the wires together once or twice to hold. Tape the wires together for a stem. (See Plate 71.)

NYLON NET FLUFF: A nylon net fluff may be used to advantage by wiring it into the corsage as you need a space filled, or a note of color. It is simply a little fluff of net wired on a stem. The simplest one to make uses a three-inch square of net, gathered straight across the center and held with one hand. Wrap the middle of an eight-inch piece of fine wire around the gathers and twist the wire tightly as close to the net as you can get it. The wire ends should be of equal length and are taped from close to the net to the end of the wires, just as a pod or seed would be taped. For an example of a corsage that uses several of these fluffs, see Turnip Slice Calla Lily Corsage, (Plate 73.)

RIBBON POINTS: Here are two kinds of ribbon points that will add interest to your corsages. Both are bits of ribbon with a wire stem. To make "rabbit ears," wrap a fine wire around the middle of a three- to four-inch piece of ribbon with both ends cut on a bias. Twist the wire tightly. In taping the wire stem, start just a bit above the wire on the ribbon, pulling both halves of the ribbon together to form the "rabbit ears," Fig. 44 (A).

The second ribbon point shown in (B) is also made with about 4″ of ribbon. Holding one end of the ribbon in each hand, bring

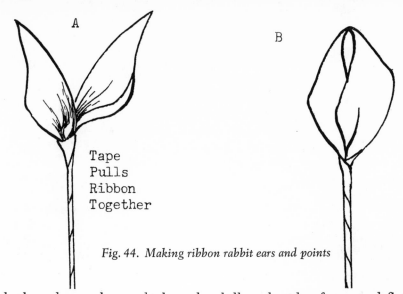

A

B

Tape
Pulls
Ribbon
Together

Fig. 44. Making ribbon rabbit ears and points

both ends together and place the dull underside of one end flat against the shiny outer side of the other end. This will form a little conical peak which you pinch flat. Wire and tape the two ends together exactly as for the "rabbit ears" point. (Used in top Corn Cob Flower Corsage, Plate 68.)

BOW: The bow, which should not dominate the other materials, is added after the rest of the corsage is finished. Tape a piece of fine wire in a harmonizing color, pass it around the bow, and twist it to hold the loops of ribbon in place. Tape this wire stem into the corsage stem, too, unless you want to change the bow later. In this case, just twist the bow stem two or three times around the corsage stem for easy removal in the future. If you prefer all natural materials, make a long-lasting, interest-provoking bow using fresh cornhusks or leaves. To use the leaves, rip the heavy midrib out and allow the leaf to wilt for about 24 hours. Fashion it into a bow and fasten with wire. Attach it to corsage where it will dry slowly to a grey-green or tan color, and it will probably last for a very long time (I have some that lasted four years.) Gladiolus or iris foliage may also be used for bows.

SPRAY: All corsages or other decorations and arrangements made of dried plant materials are benefited by one or two coats of clear plastic or acrylic spray which may be purchased at any paint shop. It will bring out hidden color and give all materials (except ribbon, nylon net or chenille stems) a clean, finished look without a high gloss. It also helps to preserve the material and strengthens most fragile materials.

191

Plate 68. Corncob three-petaled flower corsage

Plate 67. Corncob flower corsage with five single flowers

CORNCOB FLOWER CORSAGES

These examples show how corncobs, husks and kernels can be used effectively to make corsages.

Single Flowers

Materials Needed

> 5 slices dried corncob, ½" thick, 1" diameter for flowers
> 5 items such as date pit, hemlock cone, bee balm seed head, artificial red berry, corn kernel for centers
> 2 or 3 cornhusks for leaves
> 3 date pits
> 6 tufts white pine needles for background
> ¾ yd. vari-colored corsage ribbon
> #30 wire, 9" to 12" long
> Tape and clear plastic spray

192

STEP 1. Wire all five items that will be used for centers. (See Strange Flowers, Wiring.)

STEP 2. With a corsage pin or darning needle, pierce a hole in the center of each corncob slice; run the wire stem of one of the centers through this hole. Apply a bit of cement around the wire on the cob slice and pull wire down so that center rests firmly on the slice. Make all five flowers this way, and hang, heads down, until cement is dry.

STEP 3. Cut four leaf shapes of appropriate size for the cob flowers out of cornhusks, with the grain of the husk running vertically from tip of leaf to stem. Gather one end and tape it. Then wire it and tape the stem. Do all four and lay them aside.

STEP 4. Separately wire and tape each of the six white pine needle tufts. Wire and tape the three date pits.

STEP 5. Starting with the flowers, add pine needle tufts for background and date pits for contrast of form; tape all these stems together at one point with one or two twists of tape. Spray with plastic spray and finally, add the ribbon bow. (Plate 67.)

Three-Petaled Flower

Materials Needed

> 3 slices dried corncob, ½″ thick, for flower
> 5 kernels colored corn, for center
> Cornhusks, for leaves
> 1½ yds. narrow ribbonzene
> #32 wire
> Tape and clear plastic spray

This corsage is made of a three-petaled corncob flower with a center of blue kernels from squaw corn. Four cornhusk leaves and a blue bow to match the kernels complete the ornament. Plate 68.

STEP 1. Make the flower following instructions for basic petaled flower in chapter V, *Strange Flowers*.

STEP 2. Make leaves using a wide strip of husk gathered with the grain of husk running from side to side.

STEP 3. Arrange the leaves around the flowers and tape all stems together at one point. Spray with plastic spray and add ribbon.

NORWAY SPRUCE CONE PETAL FLOWERS

Cones are another of the so-useful corsage materials. In the corsage shown here, the arborvitae cones are used just as they grew, while the Norway spruce cones have supplied the single scales that make up the three five-petaled flowers. Enough of the core of the cone adheres to the scale so that no other center is necessary for the flowers. (Plate 69, Top.)

Materials Needed

> 15 Norway spruce cone scales (core of cone left on) for flowers
> 6 arborvitae cones
> 4 chinaberry seeds for buds
> 9 podocarpus leaves
> 1 small lion's tail (leonotis)
> ¾ yd. ribbon
> Picture cord wire
> Tape and clear plastic spray

STEP 1. Make three cone flowers following directions in Strange Flowers, Basic Petaled flower, with these exceptions:

No separate center. The bits of core of the cone that adhere to the scale when pulling it off the cone become the center.

Use two wires instead of one in each cone scale. Drill two small holes in each scale near the pointed end and put one wire through each hole. This will give better control of the petal.

STEP 2. Individually wire and tape the remaining material. For the slender, curving lines, wire the nine grey-green podocarpus leaves with extra-fine wire. Six arborvitae cones and the small green lion's tail form the center of interest. Four chinaberry seeds, which have a natural hole in them, become the buds. Cement two wires in the holes, and tape the wires.

STEP 3. Assemble all parts into a pleasing design, spray with clear plastic spray and add a ribbon bow. In this case, a two-faced satin ribbon, one side medium brown, the other grey-green, harmonizes beautifully with the medium brown tones of the seeds, the arborvitae cones and the cone scale flowers.

Plate 69. Norway spruce cone scale corsage (top) and kapok blossom calyx corsage (bottom)

KAPOK BLOSSOM CALYX FLOWERS

Each flower in this corsage is the calyx from a kapok blossom with a center added. Kapok trees grow only in a small part of the country, so if they don't grow in your area, you can purchase the blossom calyxes from a shop dealing in dried plant materials. The corsage is a good example of the imaginative use of unusual material: the baptisia pods are black, as is the outside of the calyxes, while the inside, or flower petals, is a soft, fuzzy tan. Yellow stamens, red seed centers, and a bow that changes as you move from yellow to green to brown complete this most effective combination of colors and plant material. (Plate 69, Bottom.)

Materials Needed

5 kapok blossom calyxes
1 bunch artificial yellow flower stamens
5 red sandalwood seeds
11 baptisia pods
¾ yd. ribbon
Cement
#28 wire
Tape and shellac (Do *not* shellac kapok calyxes)

STEP 1. Each kapok calyx has a large center hole. Drill two small holes across from each other near the edges of the center hole. Put a wire down through both holes, crossing the large center hole to do it, and twist the two wires together up tightly to the calyx; tape the wire stem for about 1″. Wire and tape all five calyxes.

STEP 2. Take a small bunch of stamens (about 12). Fold in the middle; wire and tape the folded end (this makes 24 yellow ends for each center). With fingers, spread the stamens to lay flat in a circle and cement the red sandalwood seeds in the center.

STEP 3. Draw the wire stem of the center down through the opening in the calyx and tape all wires together. Make five of these flowers.

STEP 4. Wire the 11 baptisia pods. Use narrow tape to wrap the wires down to the ends. (See Strange Flowers, Wiring and Taping.) Shellac and hang to dry.

Step 5. Assemble two flowers and five pods in one unit, taping all stems together to make a single long stem. Lay aside. Assemble the remaining flowers and pods into a second unit, taping all wires together into one long stem.

Step 6. Place both units together with one wire stem going up and the other stem down. Tape together in the center with one or two turns of tape. Attach bow in center.

ONION SKIN CORSAGE

Onion skins, pinecones and a bit of ribbon — what an unlikely combination! Yet when they are combined, a most delicate and delightful corsage is the result. (Plate 70.)

Plate 70. Onion skin corsage

Materials Needed

> 5 onion skin flowers (See Strange Flowers.)
> 5 sugar pinecone scales for leaves
> ¾ yd. ribbon
> #32 wire
> Tape and shellac for scales

STEP 1. Wire and tape the five pinecone scales (See Strange Flowers, Wiring Hard Items Without Stems.) Shellac them and let dry.

STEP 2. Assemble flowers and leaves into a pleasing design. Tape at just one point, where all wires come together near the center. Spread stems and cut to varying lengths. Add a matching satin bow.

PEANUT SHUCK CORSAGE

Never throw away your peanut shucks! Save those that didn't crack or tear as the peanuts were broken in half. This particular corsage was made for holiday wear. The peanut shuck flowers are in a soft orchid color with a light sprinkling of orchid-colored glitter. Nylon net of a deeper color is the background and a satin bow in several values of orchid completes this exciting color harmony. (Plate 71.)

Materials Needed

> 5 whole peanuts (matched for size and split carefully in half on the natural line of division) for flowers
> 6 whole small peanuts for leaves and flower centers
> ½ yd. nylon net (about 5" wide) for backing
> ¾ yd. ribbon
> About 30-32 pieces picture cord wire 9" long
> Tape and shellac
> Glitter and glitter glue

STEP 1. Make two peanut shuck flowers as directed in the chapter on Strange Flowers, with this exception: Carefully pierce two holes in the bottom of each peanut shuck and wire it with two pieces of fine wire (two wires reduce the chance of their pulling through the soft peanut shuck). Also note that the six small, round peanuts are pierced and wired straight across through one end. After they have been wired, dip all peanuts and shucks in shellac and hang to dry.

Step 2. Make a nylon net backing. See Assembling and "Dressing Up" the Corsage, at the beginning of this chapter.

Step 3. Assemble the two flowers and the whole peanuts as shown, into a good design. Add nylon net in back, fanning it out to form a soft background for the peanut units.

Step 4. Spray entire corsage with glitter glue and quickly sprinkle glitter on lightly. Add bow.

Plate 71. Peanut corsage

PARTY RYE BREAD CORSAGE

As a conversation piece, nothing can equal a corsage made of slices of party rye bread. The medium dark brown of the nylon net backing and the rust brown satin bow accent the soft tan and brown tones of the flowers. (Plate 72.)

Materials Needed

    2 slices party rye bread for flowers
    2 hemerocallis seed pods for centers
    6 silverleaf leaves (or bottlebrush or melaleuca leaves)
    4" square nylon net, medium dark brown
    Ribbon
    #32 wire
    Tape and shellac

Step 1. Make two party rye bread flowers. (See Strange Flowers). The corsage illustrated here has hemerocallis seedpods for centers.

199

STEP 2. Make nylon net backing by gathering the net down through the center with the fingers and wrapping a piece of wire very tightly twice around the gathers. Twist the wire close to the net to hold. Tape the wire stem.

STEP 3. Wire and tape each of the six silverleaf leaves separately (see Strange Flowers — How to Wire and Tape.)

STEP 4. Assemble flowers and leaves into a triangular design and add the nylon net unit in back of the bread flowers. Tape all stems together from right under the lower flower to the ends. All stems should be cut to about 2½". Add bow.

Plate 72. Party rye bread corsage

CORSAGE OF TURNIP AND CATTAIL CALLA LILIES

It is unlikely that any turnip before now has found itself intentionally on milady's lapel. Yet here it is, dried to a soft yellow color, with a fluff of yellow nylon net and a yellow bow to give it glamour. (Plate 73.)

Materials Needed

    3 slices dried yellow turnip, for the lily
    3 small cattails, 2" long, for spadix or center
    3 eleagnus leaves
    1 hemlock cone
    ¾ yd. ribbon
    Nylon net
    #30 wire
    Tape and cement

Plate 73. Turnip and cattail calla lily corsage

STEP 1. Make three turnip and cattail calla lilies (see Strange Flowers, Dried Vegetable Slice Flower.)
STEP 2. Wire the three eleagnus leaves.
STEP 3. Arrange the three flowers and three leaves into a triangular design. Tape in position. Add nylon net and bow as shown, and cement a hemlock cone in the center of the bow.

POTATO CORSAGE

Would you consider wearing potatoes on your lapel? No? You might, if they looked like this (Plate 74.)

Single Slice Potato Flowers

Materials Needed

8 square potato slices for flowers
8 hemlock cones for centers
Ribbon
Nylon net
#30 wire
Tape and cement

Plate 74. Two potato flower corsages

STEP 1. Make eight single slice flowers with hemlock cone centers (See Strange Flowers, Potato Flower.)

STEP 2. Assemble the flowers into a pleasing design and tape the stems together. Add a nylon net backing and a bow. (See Assembling and "Dressing Up" the Corsage, Backing and Ribbon, beginning of this chapter.)

Multi-Petaled Potato Flower

A potato, transformed into a translucent amber-petaled flower is a metamorphosis hard to believe.

Materials Needed

> 12 to 15 small potato slices oven-dried for flower and leaves
> Small grouping of hydrangea blossoms for center
> Ribbon
> #30 wire
> Tape

STEP 1. Make a potato flower. (See Strange Flowers, Potato Flower.)

STEP 2. Wire and tape three or four slices for leaves.

STEP 3. Assemble flower and leaves. Tape together and add bow.

202

GRAPEFRUIT RIND ROSE CORSAGE

This corsage, which uses a rose made from the inner white rind of a grapefruit and has morning glory seedpods for buds, will surely turn all eyes wherever you may wear it. (Plate 75.)

Plate 75. Grapefruit rind rose corsage

Materials Needed

Prepared grapefruit rind for rose
Morning glory pods for buds
Ribbon
#24 wire
White thread
Tape

STEP 1. Make grapefruit rind rose (see Strange Flowers, Roses.)
STEP 2. Wire and tape the three morning glory pods.
STEP 3. Hold buds and rose together in a good position and tape stems together at one point. Add bow.

TABLE DECORATIONS FROM CORSAGES

Table decorations may be made using corsages as the center of attraction. Any of the corsages shown can be used singly or in multiples for a most effective arrangement. Then when the guests leave the dining room, each lady is presented with a corsage. (Plate 76.)

Tall Centerpiece

Materials Needed

Wooden disc, 1″ thick, 8″ diameter
Wooden dowel, 18″ long, 1″ diameter
Wooden dowel, 3″ long, ¼″ diameter
Sandpaper and shellac
7 florists' water picks or orchid tubes 3½″ long
Floral tape (white) and cement
3″ x 8″ sheet of writing paper
8 or 9 corsages and 8 or 9 boutonnieres

STEP 1. For a tall centerpiece, use an 18″ wooden dowel about 1″ in diameter and an 8″ wooden disc about 1″ thick. Measure to find the exact center of the disc and drill a ¼″ hole at this point. Drill a second ¼″ hole 2″ deep in one end of the dowel. Be sure the hole does not slant in any direction or the dowel will not stand straight. Now take a 3″ piece of ¼″ dowel and push it into the hole in the large dowel. Push the other end into the flat disc to see if it fits and to see that the whole unit stands in a straight, upright position. Take apart and sand the disc until it is perfectly smooth on top and at all edges Give it a coat of shellac and set aside.

Plate 76. Corsage tall centerpiece

STEP 2. To complete the upright part of the arrangement, you will need seven florists' water picks or orchid tubes about 3½" long, white tape and a piece of writing paper about 3" x 8". Wrap the paper (long way) around the dowel on the opposite end from the hole. It should extend about 1½" above it and is held in place by a bit of cement. Now wind the whole dowel, including paper top, with white tape. Cover the entire surface and pull the tape as tight as possible so there is no chance of its slipping later. Do not draw the top opening any smaller as you tape.

STEP 3. Wind or wrap all seven water picks with tape as carefully as the dowel. Now start at the bottom and holding one pick with its bottom even with the bottom of the dowel, tape it to the dowel. Lap the tape and be sure it is smooth and even as you wrap. The pick should not slant in any direction; it must be in a vertical position.

STEP 4. Then, a little to one side, and just its own length higher than the preceding one, wrap on another taped pick. Continue in this fashion until all picks are taped on. Continue the tape to the top of the paper collar, being careful not to draw it so tight that the opening will be made smaller. This collar serves as a holder for a candle. The picks should be in a spiral around the dowel when the last one is put in position.

STEP 5. Arrange dowel and base together and paint any color you wish. One or two coats will suffice, or you may gild, silver it or add glitter.

STEP 6. Place one corsage and one boutonierre in each pick, with one or two extras lying on the base. A few sprays of evergreen, ferns, or other greenery add to the beauty. If other candles are being used on the table, the candle on top should harmonize with them. This corsage holder may be used with fresh flowers as the picks will hold enough water to keep your flowers fresh for several hours.

Low Centerpiece

A low centerpiece may be made using a piece of styrofoam, 2″ thick, and of a suitable size and shape for the table being used. Florists' green styrofoam is best for this.

Materials Needed

> Styrofoam, 2″ thick (green)
> Evergreen sprays
> Pipe cleaners
> Corsages and boutonierres

STEP 1. Arrange small evergreen sprays on the styrofoam base and hold in place by pushing small "hairpins" made of pipe cleaners over the evergreen into the styrofoam base. Two such hairpins, not more than 1″ each in length will be enough to hold each spray.

STEP 2. Place the corsages on the base in a pleasing manner. Allow at least one corsage for each lady and a small boutonierre for each of the gentlemen. Make the corsages of dried plant materials days in advance of the dinner party. Of course, all materials may be painted, dyed or glittered to suit the occasion and to match the color scheme.

HATS

Many charming hats may be fashioned from plant material. They are as practical and beautiful as many made of fabric or other materials. And of course, if you use an old discarded hat for a frame, you will be starting off in the right direction, as it will be the correct head size and a becoming shape for you.

Plate 77. Headband or coronet

HEADBAND OR CORONET

This coronet-type hat is most becoming and is enhanced by placing a net whimsy over it and fastening it in place with one or two stitches. (Plate 77.)

Materials Needed

> 5 grey sea-bean seeds
> 6 grey-green (annual) poppy pods
> 2 larch cones with tip ends cut off
> 4 small burr acorn caps
> 8 pinon pinecone scales
> 8 red kidney beans
> 4 ear pod seeds
> 6 palm seeds
> 4 Mugho pinecones
> 4 Queen's crape myrtle seedpods
> 8 blue gum eucalyptus pods
> 2 fingerhorn eucalyptus pods
> 14 grey Job's tear seeds
> 6 beech-nut burrs
> Plastic headband (from five and dime store)
> Velvet ribbon, brown
> Wire and tape

STEP 1. Each of the items listed must be given a wire stem, (see Strange Flowers, How to Wire and Tape Material). Some must have holes drilled to wire them. Cones, beech-nut and crape myrtle are the exceptions. Tape all wire stems with half-width tape.

STEP 2. Assemble these seeds and pods into a long, slender placement, taping some into clusters and adding pieces as you work down the length of it. Each seed or pod is held in place with tape. The unit should be long enough to reach from one end to the other of the plastic band. Do not attach to the headband yet.

STEP 3. Give the completed unit three or four light coats of plastic spray. Let dry thoroughly between coats.

STEP 4. Prepare the headband by covering it with a brown velvet ribbon. This is, of course, optional, but makes for a more elegant product. It is hand-stitched to, and around, the plastic band.

STEP 5. Attach the seed and pod unit onto the plastic band with stitches or with tape-covered fine wire.

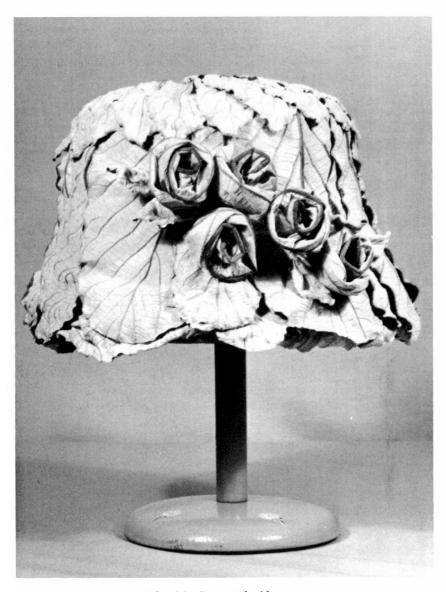

Plate 78. Cecropia leaf hat

CECROPIA LEAF HAT

Another hat is made out of cecropia leaves. These are large tropical leaves, white on the underside and when dry, either green or brown on the upper side. (Plate 78.)

Materials Needed

Hat frame
2 or 3 medium-to-large cecropia leaves
Cement
#30 wire
Tape

STEP 1. To make the dry cecropia leaves soft and pliable, place them in warm water for a few minutes; then shake out the excess water and roll them up in a slightly damp towel. Put aside for 15 to 30 minutes.

STEP 2. Prepare your hat frame by binding the rim with a bias strip of suitable color material. This should cover the rim about two inches both inside and outside.

STEP 3. Cut the moist leaves into sections following the lines of natural division. Take the largest lobes of the leaves and place around the rim of the frame. Using a needle and white thread, hold each leaf section in place with one or two stitches over the heavy midrib and near the stem end. Lap each lobe almost halfway over the other. Remember that the leaves shrink by about 1/3 of their size in drying, so be sure to let them come well over the edge of the rim and also lap them deeply, one over the other. Attach as many rows of leaf sections around the hat as are needed for good coverage. Cover the crown with the smaller lobes, and *cement* the last one in place to keep stitches from showing. When all are in place, hold them there until dry by putting a soft cloth band over the leaves around the crown (pin in place) and laying a folded towel on the top to keep the leaves from curling out of shape.

STEP 4. To make the five rosebuds used for trim, take a large leaf section and fold along the midrib. At the pointed (stem) end, turn down at right angles for about 1½″. Now roll into a bud shape, gathering the double edges at the bottom as you go. Fasten the gathered edge with several twists of wire. Pull wire tight. Two #30 wires are used for each bud. Cut off excess leafage below the wire. Let dry. Cut the tips off three or four small lobes and wire at the cut end for rose leaves. When dry, tape all stems (see Strange Flowers, Wiring and Taping.)

STEP 5. Assemble the five rosebuds and the leaves into a single unit, corsage fashion.

210

STEP 6. When the leaves are dry, remove towel and cloth from hat. If necessary, use a few dabs of cement to hold leaf edges in place. Add rosebuds and secure them with a few stitches.

Plate 79. Pampas grass hat

PAMPAS GRASS HAT

Pampas grass was used to cover this frame. The grass is in green, orange and natural straw colors.

Materials Needed

> Hat frame
> 3 stems pampas or plume grass
> Cement
> Net whimsy (nylon net or tulle)
> Velvet ribbon for bows

STEP 1. Remove the main stem from the grass plume. Make small groupings of tufts, keeping the small stems, which should be cut to about ½" or less, even at the one end. Fasten the tufts to the bottom edge of the hat frame with one or two stitches or cement, allowing some of the grass to extend beyond the edge. Make a row all around the bottom edge in this manner.

STEP 2. Cover the entire frame with the tufts of grass, working evenly around the hat from the lower part up to the crown. When covered, go back to the bottom row and cement the tips of the tufts to the underside of the rim.

STEP 3. When completed, cover the grass with a very soft, neutral color nylon net or tulle to hold it in place. Attach a sequined nylon whimsy and velvet bows, if desired. Stitch through the velvet bows to the center crown.

SEED JEWELRY

Here, indeed, is an unlimited field for your fertile imagination — costume jewelry to suit milady's every whim!

Some of the smaller materials you have been saving and collecting will be ideal for this purpose. Indian or squaw corn, which you can grow yourself or purchase in almost any florist shop in the fall, has a wonderful color range and requires little in the way of tools to fashion the lovely kernels into pins, corsages, earrings, etc. Melon or cantaloupe seeds are usually a little off-white, but if you prefer a brighter color, they take food colors very well. The seeds from the pumpkin and Hubbard squash can be made into very smart jewelry. Squash seeds are a little whiter and larger in size. They may be painted with ordinary enamel paint or tinted with food or shoe dyes. A coat of shellac is necessary to keep the dyes or colors from rubbing off.

The findings (pin backs, earring clips and silver chains) may be purchased at five and dime stores or hobby shops. To obtain a high gloss in imitation of ceramic jewelry, give each item at least one coat of very heavy gloss varnish. For a less glossy finish, use lacquer. This comes in both dull and glossy finish.

For adding color, use a good enamel paint of your chosen color. Brush it on. Use two coats if one does not produce the intensity of color you want.

Remember that your friends, and indeed everyone who sees your jewelry, will want a closer look, so be sure to do really good work with extra care on taping and wiring and cementing; no messy lumps, no ends of wire sticking out. You will undoubtedly be called upon to create more jewelry to give to friends and relatives.

Two basic methods for making most seed jewelry are:

A. Cementing seeds individually on a background in a pleasing pattern.

B. Wiring and taping seeds individually and assembling into an interesting design.

JEWELRY MADE USING CEMENTING METHOD

Corn Kernel and Cantaloupe Seed Pins and Earrings

One of the easiest-to-make seed jewelry projects uses corn kernels and cantaloupe seeds cemented to a plastic disc background. (Plate 80A.)

Plate 80. Corn kernel and cantaloupe seed pins and earrings

Materials Needed

> Corn kernels from Indian or squaw corn
> Cantaloupe seeds (dyed, if desired)
> Poppy seeds
> Plastic discs (1″ to 2″ diameter) or buttons, flat on both sides
> Jewelry findings (pinbacks, earwires, etc.)
> Cement and cotton
> Shellac

STEP 1. Select corn kernels for the color you want. Try to choose only the flat regular shaped kernels for petals. When you pull the kernel off the ear of corn, it has a little white tuft on the end. Cut this tuft off with a razor blade. In selecting kernels for flower centers, use kernels that are more round as you look at them on the cob.

213

STEP 2. Put a generous dab of cement on the center of the plastic disc you are using as a background. Arrange five corn kernel petals on the disc, leaving a space for the center kernel.

STEP 3. Saturate a small wad of cotton in cement and place it in the center space. Put center kernel in on top of cotton, which helps it to sit right. Set piece aside and dry for ½ hour.

It's more fun to work on several pieces of jewelry at once; then when one has to dry, you can be working on another.

STEP 4. Put a drop of cement on each melon seed as you set it in place on the disc. These seeds, too, must be left ½ hour to dry.

STEP 5. Glue pinback on back of piece and let dry thoroughly. Give the whole piece a protective coating of shellac.

Another corn kernel and cantaloupe seed variation is shown in Plate 80(B). The method of making it is exactly the same. The differences are: Background is flat ring instead of disc. Flowers have three petals — not five and there are two cantaloupe seed leaves for each flower.

To make the pleasant textured background, wait until the piece is complete and the cement thoroughly dry. Shellac the area to be textured using a very small brush. While shellac is still wet, sprinkle poppy seeds over the piece. They will cling only where there is wet shellac.

The matching earrings in Plate 80(C), have a small disc or button base, and are made in the same fashion.

There are almost as many variations of corn kernel flowers as there are kernels of corn. Flowers can be made with three, four, or five petals and you have a choice of natural colors ranging from an off-white through yellow, burnt-orange, and many shades of lavender and brown.

The design can be changed by cutting a different shaped background from a sheet of plastic and adding melon seeds, radish pods, popcorn kernels, poppy seeds, date pits; in fact, almost any seed or pod.

SUNFLOWER SEED PENDANT OR PIN AND EARRINGS

This pretty matched set would make a thoughtful gift, if you can bear to part with it. Better still, make two sets. (Plate 81.)

214

Plate 81. Sunflower seed pendant (or pin) and earrings

Materials Needed

Sunflower seeds
3 red sandalwood seeds for centers
3 plastic discs, 1 for pendant, 2 for earrings
Pinback and 1 pair earwires
Cement and cotton
Shellac

STEP 1. Cement sunflower seeds to plastic discs. For the pin, start by placing the outer row first to cover the edge of the disc. Let cement dry. Then work in toward the center, letting cement dry as necessary.

STEP 2. Cement in center seed. Let dry.

STEP 3. Cement on pin-back and earwires. For the pendant, make a hole in plastic disc and insert a wire ring for chain.

JEWELRY MADE USING WIRING METHOD

Corn Kernel Flowers

This delightful spray pin can be made with its own attached pin on back, or you can pin it to your lapel with a corsage pin. It is made with the wiring technique. (See Fig. 45.)

Materials Needed

> Corn kernels
> Date pits
> Picture cord wire
> Floratape
> Cement and cotton
> Pin back or corsage pin
> Shellac

Wiring Kernels

STEP 1. Pierce each kernel with a large darning needle, (A). Put a fine wire (6" long) through hole, (B). Pull the two ends together and twist wire two or three times snugly up against kernel, (C). For this pin, wire seven kernels this way. Also wire two date pits the same way. Take three wired kernels and hold together in position. Twist all three wire stems tightly together, (D). Cut floral tape in half lengthwise to give ¼" width. Wrap tape two or three times around stem just beneath the kernels to start it. Push this tightly up against kernels and wrap smoothly to end of stem, (E). Make two three-petal flowers this way. Then glue in centers using small wad of cotton as in previous projects. Take last single-wired kernel. Put tape around stem in same way, leaving small corner extending up onto kernel to form calyx of bud, (F). Wrap date pits in the same way.

STEP 2. ASSEMBLE: You should now have the pieces shown in (G). Tape a flower and a bud together as in (H). Add another flower and tape it into position (I). Last, tape in the two date pit leaves, (I). For the pin, use as narrow a pin-back as possible. Flatten stem section slightly where pin is to be attached. Cement on pin-back. When cement is dry, you may wrap more tape around stem and pin-back for additional strength. If you don't want to attach a pin-back, simply pin the flower spray to your lapel with a corsage pin. Finally, give the whole piece a coat of shellac to make it more durable.

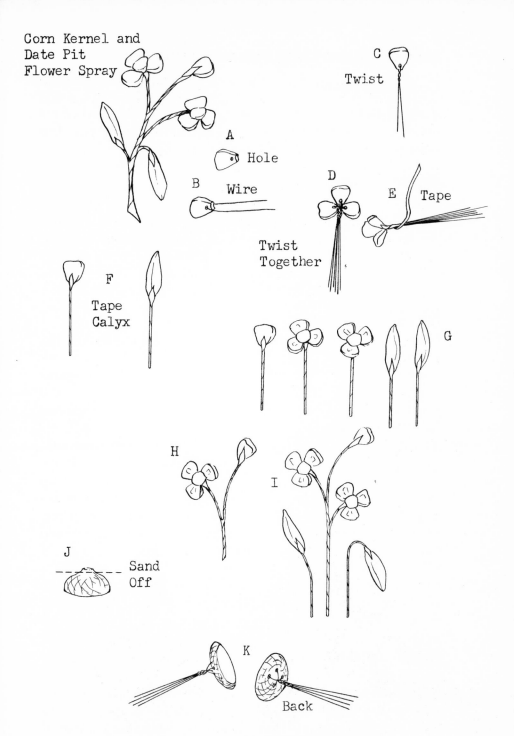

Corn Kernel and
Date Pit
Flower Spray

C Twist

A ⬠ Hole

B Wire

D Twist Together

E Tape

F Tape Calyx

G

H

I

J ⬚ Sand Off

K Back

Fig. 45. Making corn kernel, date pit and acorn flowers

ACORN AND DATE PITS PIN AND DRESS CLIP

Once the techniques of wiring and assembling the individual parts of each flower is mastered, there is very little instruction that can be given.

In working with acorn caps, however, this procedure should be followed: (See Fig. 45.) Break off the stem as close to the cap as you can and sand the rest down flat (J). It is also important that the caps be wired with two wires (K) which gives them more stability. In general, the acorn cap and all the larger pieces are wired and taped individually, and then taped together to make up the design you want. Smaller decorative parts, centers, edgings, etc., are usually glued into position. (Plate 82.) Jewelry findings will hold better if they are both glued and taped. This is usually possible on a pin-back, but earring backs can only be glued.

Materials Needed

    Acorn caps
    Date pits
    Orange-dyed cantaloupe seeds
    Black hemerocallis seeds
    Picture cord wire
    Floratape
    Pin back
    Dress clip back
    Cement and shellac

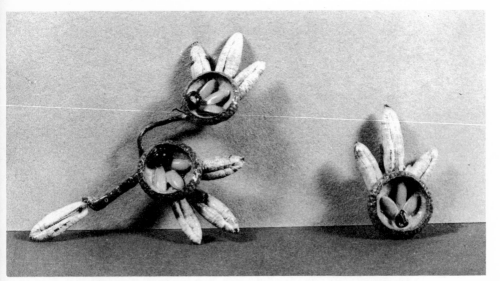

Plate 82. Acorn and date pit pin and dress clip

218

Step 1. Individually wire and tape acorn caps and date pits as in Corn Kernel and Date Pit instructions.

Step 2. Assemble into units, one acorn cap and three date pits taped together for each unit. Arrange units as desired and tape stems together.

Step 3. Cement cantaloupe and hemerocallis seed design in acorn caps and let dry.

Step 4. Cement pin-back in place and let dry. Add tape to strengthen pin-back and shellac whole piece. For dress clip, turn the wire stem of the acorn and date pit unit under the piece and attach to dress clip back, to make as little bulk as possible.

ACORN AND BULL-HORN ACACIA SET

There's a primitive note in the design of this set that should make a good sports accessory. (Plate 83.)

Materials Needed

    Acorn caps
    Spines from bull-horn acacia
    Bittersweet berry seed pod
    Bittersweet berries
    26 gauge copper wire
    Cement
    Shellac

Step 1. Wrap copper wire tightly and close together four to six times around one horn of acacia spine. Continuing with same piece of wire, bring it over to other horn and wrap evenly the same as the first. Snip wire and tuck end under in back where it won't show. The wire between the two horns forms a kind of brace against which the acorn cap will rest. Wire two more spines the same way for earrings.

Step 2. For pendant, wrap another piece of copper wire around several times where the horns join, and extend it up to form a loop for a chain.

Step 3. Using small bits of cotton saturated in cement, set the acorn caps in position and let dry.

Step 4. Cement a bittersweet seed pod and berry inside each acorn cap and let dry. For earrings, cement earwires on back after other cement is dry.

Step 5. When all cement is dry, apply a protective coating of shellac.

Plate 83. Acorn and bull-horn acacia pendant and earrings

PUMPKIN AND CRABEYE SEED JEWELRY

White pumpkin seed petals and red and black crabeye seed centers make a striking color contrast in this flower spray. A few individual pumpkin seeds and crabeye seeds form the buds at the tips of the spray. White floral tape was used throughout, and an ample bow of both red and white narrow ribbon completes the picture. (Plate 84, Fig. 46.)

Materials Needed

Pumpkin or Hubbard squash seeds
Crabeye seeds
Picture-cord wire
#26 florist's wire
White floral tape
Red and white ribbon ½" wide
Corsage pin
Cement and cotton

STEP 1. Using the same wiring techniques as for a preceding project, Corn Kernel Flowers, individually wire and tape approximately 45 pumpkin seeds. Group these wired and taped seeds into five-petaled flowers and tape the wires together. Make eight flowers and four or five buds. Where extra length or strength is needed, tape a piece of #26 wire into the stem (A).

STEP 2. Drill holes in one end of four crabeye seeds, then wire and tape each one for a bud. *Caution — Do not leave any drilled crabeye seeds where children can get at them.* Though the unbroken seed could be swallowed and passed harmlessly through the body, the crushed or pierced seed is quite poisonous if eaten. So do be careful. Place a small dab of cotton saturated in cement into the center of each flower and set three crabeye seeds in for the center. Let cement dry.

STEP 3. Make two groups of flowers (B) and tape the two groups together, leaving three stem ends extending on each side to add strength of line to the design. Cover the joining with a narrow ribbon bow. The corsage may be pinned on with a regular corsage pin.

Earrings — Single flowers may be made into matching earrings. These should be glued, not wired, using a small plastic disc as a base.

Plate 84. Pumpkin and crabeye seed spray and earrings

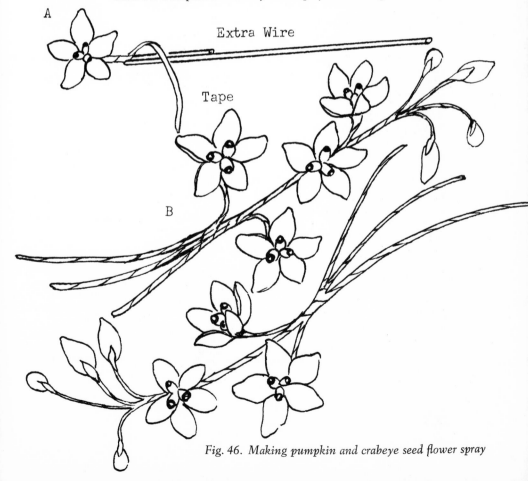

A

Extra Wire

Tape

B

Fig. 46. Making pumpkin and crabeye seed flower spray

INDEX

222

224